# FLYING KITES

## by James Wagenvoord

The Macmillan Company, New York

"A curious experience executed by M. D. Colladon near Cologny with the aid of a kite in 1844"

Library of Congress Catalog Card Number: 68-31281

First Printing

The Macmillan Company, New York
Collier-Macmillan Canada Ltd., Toronto, Ontario

Printed in the United States of America

ACKNOWLEDGMENTS

◆ This book began on a spring evening in 1967 when Grace and Charlie Glass fed me a dinner and Charlie, a cartoonist and advertising writer, blurted out self-consciously that he had taken up kiteflying. Since that evening it seems as though everyone I have met is either a kiteflyer or "knows one." Most have been helpful in putting the book together. Such kiteflyers as Bob Ingraham of the American Kitefliers Association, Paul Garber of the National Air Museum, Surendra Bahadur, George Kelly, Al Hartig, Frank Rodriquez, Ulis Sines, Frank Lorenzo, Paul Freeman, and dozens of others have gone out of their way to make material available. A special debt of gratitude is owed to Tomi Ungerer, who made his outstanding files on turn-of-the-century kiteflying available and then managed to track down a copy of an almost impossible-to-find book, *Les Cerf-volants*, in a Paris toy shop, and to Mrs. Vera Cassilly of the National Geographic Society, who really introduced me to Alexander Graham Bell's magnificent kites. Two people deserve public thanks for tolerance, let alone assistance—Howard Sandum, who edited the book, and Julia Coopersmith of Brandt and Brandt, my agent and attractive human wailing wall. And if anyone enjoys this book it is largely because of Anita Laidman, who, in addition to assisting with the research, drawing the Folio diagrams, and working with Dennis Wheeler on the graphic design, never ceased being a woman and a kiteflyer.
JAMES WAGENVOORD

My advice in the midst of all the seriousness, is to keep an eye out for the tinker's shuffle, the flying of kites, and kindred sources of amusement.—**Dr. Jerome S. Bruner,** *On Knowing: Essays for the Left Hand*

# CONTENTS

# Preface

◆ Kites and kiteflyers have a history, but it isn't purely chronological. Although people have been flying kites for more than three thousand years, each new year contains all of the elements of all time. No kite has ever been made obsolete, and the basic kite, two sticks and a light fabric covering, continues to be sent up at the end of a string. The experience, the frustration of trying to make something fly, and the sheer fun of succeeding, remains fresh and successfully resists sophistication and posturing.

Adults tend to deal conversationally with kites in terms of children's fun, but every year when the weather is warm and the wind is soft, millions of children discover, while watching grown-ups, that the bigger and older one is, the easier it is to keep a hand on the kite string.

This is a book about a number of people of all ages, interests, and directions who have at least two things in common. They like kites, and they share a broad smile. When they send their kites up in search of the wind, they give nearly every air-breathing person whose eyes spot the kites floating in the sky, a brief return to a much simpler time—a time when it wasn't considered necessary to be conscious or apologetic about fun. It's difficult to be self-conscious when your eyes are fixed on a kite moving with the wind and the sky. It's a lot easier just to let a smile happen.

# More than a Fad

◆ Kites have been flown for nearly three thousand years. And men have been trying, for almost as long, to phrase an answer to the question of why people are fascinated with flying kites and watching kites. The late Somerset Maugham in his short story *The Kite* told of a man, a kiteflyer, who was imprisoned because of his refusal to pay alimony to his ex-wife. The marriage had broken up over a long and basic disagreement over his kiteflying, and his answer as to why he refused the payments was a not-so-simple "She broke my kite."

In the story Maugham is asked, "What d'you suppose there is in kite flying that makes the damned fool so mad about it?"

"You see I don't know a thing about flying a kite. Perhaps it gives him a sense of power as he watches it soaring towards the clouds and of mastery over the elements as he seems to bend the winds of heaven to his will. It may be that in some queer way he identifies himself with the kite flying so free and high above him, and it's as it were an escape from the monotony of life. It may be that in some dim confused way it represents an ideal of freedom and adventure. And you know, when a man once gets bitten with the virus of the ideal not all the Kings doctors and not all the Kings surgeons can rid him of it. But all this is very fanciful and I dare say it's just stuff and nonsense. I think you'd better put your problem before someone who knows a lot more about the psychology of the human animal than I."

◆ At 9 a.m. on a fresh cloudless Saturday morning in late June, two thousand people assembled in the Sheep Meadow area of New York's Central Park. They were there for kite-flying and had begun arriving at daybreak for New York's first annual Kite Day (the third first annual in as many years), presided over this time by Cousin Brucie, the new-sound disc-jockey voice of the American Broadcasting Company. By the time Cousin Brucie and the official judges were in their positions, the skyline was filled with several hundred home-made kites bobbing, darting, soaring, and occasionally sliding and plummeting out of the air and thumping into the overgrown sod. The meadow was surrounded by klieg lights put in place for the evening's scheduled appearance of Barbra Streisand, but throughout the day the park and the sky belonged to the kiteflyers.

This day and the crowd were by no means a unique demonstration of kiteflyer and builder strength. Only a few months earlier Paul Garber, curator of the National Air Museum in Washington, D.C., under the aegis of the Smithsonian Institution, coordinated the Smithsonian's first annual kite program. The series Four Saturday Afternoons in March included lectures, workshops on kite construction, and culminated with a Kite Carnival and Contest on the Mall in front of the Washington Monument. Fifteen hundred Washington kite-flyers of all ages legally fought the wind for the first time since 1892 when a law was passed forbidding kites within the District. The law, similar to ordinances passed by most cities and towns at the turn of the century when electric and telephone wires began their spread across horizons, stated that "It shall not be lawful for any person or persons to set up or fly any kite . . . in or upon or over any street, avenue, alley or open space, public enclosure or square within the limits of the city under a penalty of not more than ten dollars for each and every offense."

Although the law has seldom been enforced in Washington or in any town, its existence has been challenged many times by legislators affected by the cities' warm weather. One of the more specific attacks was delivered in 1963 by Democratic Congressman Frank Thompson, Jr., of New Jersey. Said the Representative, "It is my duty, not only as a father and a legislator, but as one who believes that the Declaration of Independence is a living document, to do all in my power to throw off this yoke of tyranny. It is time to repeal the kiteflying legislation." The particular law remains on the books, but Paul Garber, by spending several days cutting through red tape, succeeded in gaining his one-day moratorium.

Kites flying in front of the Washington Monuments and the kites dancing above Central Park, while not unique, are symbolic of a reemergence of kites and flyers throughout the United States. And Paul Garber of the Air Museum and the judges at the Cousin Brucie contest have all played active and representative roles in this development. Will Yolen, the self-proclaimed "Kiteflying Champion of the World," George Kelly, partner with Surendra Bahadur in New York's Go Fly a Kite Store, and Tomi Ungerer, an artist who possesses, among his wide talents, a remarkable ability as a kite designer and builder, by their individuality and in their love of kites, are similar to a growing number of dedicated and skilled flyers who have passed beyond chronological childhood.

All-age kiteflying dipped noticeably at the turn of the century with the advent of engine-powered flight. Until the late 1950s a grown man or woman who, without children, publicly flew kites was considered pretty silly. Newspapers ran virtually the same photograph every spring with the caption "Go Fly a Kite," but it slowly began to change. Men and women, who as individuals never forgot their love of paper and sticks and string and sky, became less self-conscious when seen flying kites alone. Kite contests in playgrounds and major city parks began to be for others than just children. The ten-cent-store-bought kite gave way to new designs and took advantage of new durable lightweight materials. By 1963 with the advent of the Gayla Kites one could, at prices ranging from one to five dollars, purchase a kite that would, if the string held, fly easily throughout an entire season.

Early in 1964 a group of the most dedicated and determined flyers formed the American Kitefliers Association, and the sport finally

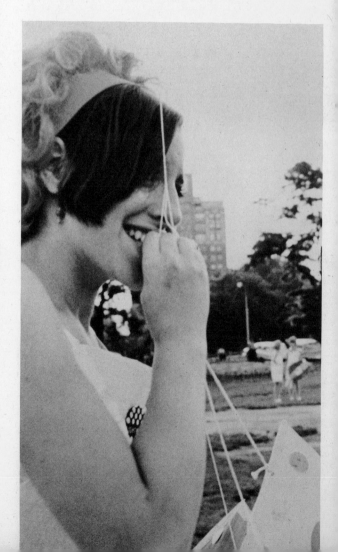

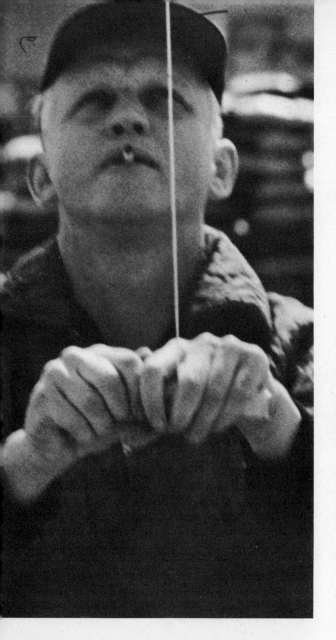

had a record center. The association's only membership requirements were five dollars and a statement that the applicant was over the age of twenty-one. Its quarterly newsletter became a focus of random and skilled flyers, and the members began corresponding with each other. The hierarchy, still virtually unknown except to their friends and other interested kiteflyers, exchanged designs and, most importantly, shared their interest. The membership list soon included such men as Walter Scott and Benn Blinn, kiteflyers from Columbus, Ohio, and Francis Rogallo, a scientist-inventor and director of experimental work in slow-speed aircraft at the National Aeronautics and Space Administration wind tunnel in Langley, Virginia. Domina Jalbert, the inventor of the Jalbert Air-Foil, as well as several other kite-form innovations used in the United States space program, and F. Rankin Weiskurber, a Detroit industrialist, who in his world travels has flown kites in most of the countries he has visited, were also among the first to become active in the association. Robert Ingraham of Silver City, New Mexico, was, with Blinn and Scott, a founder of the group and has served since its beginning as the executive secretary and editor and publisher of the magazine.

As organization began to creep into the world of kites, the individuality of the flyers and the kites themselves became more noticeable. The traditional two-stick kite form has become outnumbered in many open skies by winged boxes, dart-shaped floaters, and diamond-shaped fighter kites. As these "new" kites have gained in popularity, the flyers have become increasingly aware of the "new" kites' ancient sources and the sport's equally old traditions, and the flyers have continued to ask themselves why men fly kites. No one seems to have succeeded in phrasing an answer. But there is no question that something intensely personal does happen, the imagination is sometimes captured, and time falls away.

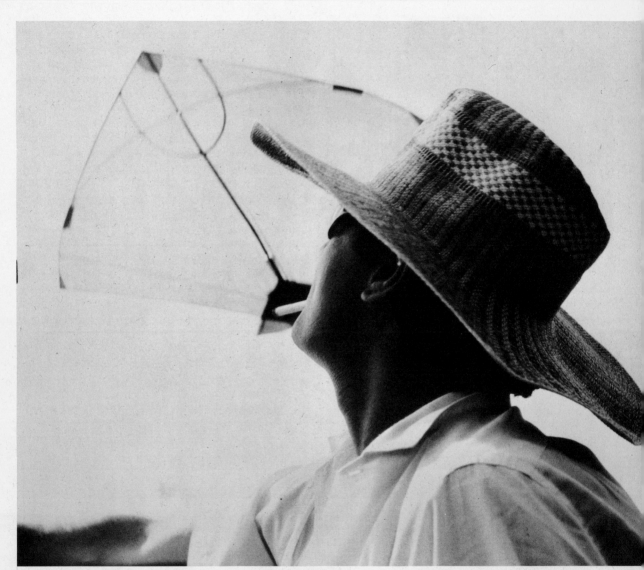
Surendra Bahadur launching an Indian fighting kite

Kites became more than a fad for George Kelly when he met Surendra Bahadur in Bombay in 1959. Having worked for two years as an Associated Press reporter in Philadelphia, he had traveled to India with the thought of working as a free-lance journalist. Instead he soon became interested in the country's handicrafts and decided to import a number of items into the United States.

The Indian fighter kite, flown with near perfection by Bahadur, was a major cause of the shift in interest. For hundreds of years kiteflying has been a favored sport for Indians of all ages. In nearly every town throughout the country a single diamond-shaped kite rising from a rooftop is a signal that another kite will soon follow, issuing a challenge to a duel. The kites, pulling at the end of strings coated with paste containing powdered glass, are maneuvered toward each other, the strings cross, a kite attempts to dash out of danger, and within a split second it is falling free, its string cut by its opponent.

The art of Indian kite fighting and the maneuverability and form of the kites captured Kelly's imagination, and a partnership was formed with Bahadur. Returning to New York, George Kelly began the job of distributing the kites shipped in by Bahadur. He also

George Kelly in the Go Fly a Kite Store

The kite stand in Central Park

began working at New York University as an electron microscopist and for the next six years alternated between electrons and kites. In the spring of 1964 Surendra moved from India to the United States, and the two young men opened up the Go Fly a Kite Store in a small artist's gallery on New York's East Side. Surendra began flying the fighting kites on weekends in the city's parks, and within a few months the store and the two men became the subject of stories in newspapers and magazines. Thomas P. F. Hoving was beginning his brief and colorful tenure as the commissioner of New York's parks, and Hoving "happenings" were becoming known throughout the country. Although there had been kiteflyers in the parks, until Tom Hoving became interested in the sport, the flyers had been unreeling their string in opposition to a standard turn-of-the-century anti-kite law. Two Hoving "happenings" changed the horizon. Kelly and Bahadur staged the first in Brooklyn's Prospect Park under the sponsorship of the Parks Department and handed a fighter kite string to the commissioner. The results were a second kite day a few weeks later in Central Park and the permanent lifting of a seventy-year-old restriction on mid-city flying.

Since that time kiteflyers and their kites have become an element of any good "city" day. In 1967 the Go Fly a Kite Store became a year-round enterprise and a meeting place for thousands of people of all ages who rediscovered an easier time. The Park Meadow is filled with people and with kites of every conceivable shape and color on the weekends, and on most Saturdays and Sundays George Kelly sets up the kite stand, unfurls Japanese fish wind banners, and begins stringing kites for surprisingly relaxed city dwellers. Surendra Bahadur, almost always wearing white duck slacks, a white shirt, his broad-brimmed hat, and sunglasses, moves smoothly across the meadow maneuvering his small kite in figure eights, bouncing it along the tops of a line of trees, and helping out flyers who are getting their lines tangled with one another or having relaxed trouble getting their kites to take a position in the air.

Bahadur launching a friend's Brazilian kite

Bahadur, Will Yolen, and Thomas P. F. Hoving at the official opening of Central Park to kiteflyers

◆ Will Yolen has flown kites all of his life. Living in the New York area, enjoying a successful career as a public relations executive, and loving kites put him in a position to become one of the most widely known kiteflyers in the country. The title "World Champion" was added to his flying credentials in 1959. He announced that he was the "New Champion" after returning from a tiger hunt with friends in India. The fly-off reportedly took place on the grounds of the palace of the Maharajah of Bharatpur. A challenge issued by the Maharajah was accepted by Yolen. After several hours of man-against-man flying, the Maharajah had his kite reeled in by a servant and saluted Will Yolen as "the new world's champion." Since very few American kiteflyers had even considered the possibility of an "old champion," the announcement was greeted with mixed emotion.

Through the years the Yolen living legend has included such apocryphal high points as the defeat of Pablo Diablo, the evil kiteflyer of Central Park. Pablo, who, according to Yolen, had been cutting down innocent kites with his glassed line, was taken on and dispatched after a six-hour flying battle over the park. Pablo Diablo has never again bothered kiteflyers. Will Yolen's greatest general public notice, however, came in the fall of 1963 when he was arrested in Central Park for flying a kite that towed an eight-foot-long "Vote for John Lindsay" sign. He decided to fight the law against displaying banners for political purposes in a city park, and the American Civil Liberties Union volunteered to defend him on the grounds that his constitutional freedom of expression was being abridged. The responsibility to decide for or against expression and kiteflyers fell to Judge James L. Watson. At the hearing Will Yolen spoke only two words. Judge Watson wanted to know if he used a spinner reel on the fishing rod that he uses for his kiteflying. "Regulation reel," said the champion. John Lindsay was already in office as the mayor when the court's decision in favor of Will Yolen was handed down. Will Yolen was free to fly his kites for a crowd or for himself.

He can be found flying a kite somewhere on any reasonable Saturday or Sunday. If a kite contest is on in the area, he's there, judging, demonstrating his fishing-pole and tuna-reel style of relatively effortless kiteflying, and occasionally answering questions from fellow kiteflyers, with a question.

"Hey, Champ, how come you don't make your own kites?"

"Did Babe Ruth make his own bats?"

Will Yolen putting a kite into the air

Lawrence Clark, Phoebe Ungerer, and Tomi Ungerer

◆ Tomi Ungerer has always made his own kites. He has also written and illustrated his own books, painted his own paintings, sculpted his own sculpture, produced his own films, and, since coming to the United States from Europe as a young artist in 1955, become successful and respected in all of his fields. His reintroduction to kites, a pastime that he knew as a child in Strasbourg, France, came during a summer in East Hampton, Long Island. He bought a small kite, flew it, and became fascinated again with the subject and the feeling. Working with a burst of energy, he began designing and building his own structures, and before the summer was over he had completed more than one hundred flying kites of all sizes and shapes, and acrylic-painted designs.

The long, white sand beaches of eastern Long Island are constantly swept by winds and are backed by miles and miles of sand dunes. During the summer of 1960 they became the setting for Tomi Ungerer's big, yet delicate, kites. Tomi Ungerer is a professional and when he takes on a subject, whether it is kites or a new medium, he goes into it with a high degree of thoroughness and zeal that matches the joy that he takes from it. He spent three summers researching, experimenting, designing, and building his kites—for the fun of building something, and for the exhilaration of watching something, which he had made, perform.

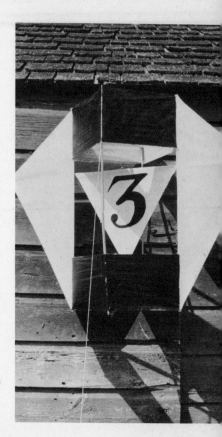

And his kites, with their intricate and complicated shapes (double and triple wings, cylindrical bodies, box forms, and tetrahedral cells) do perform. With his well-developed sense of creation and innovation, his main competition is with himself. A successful Ungerer kite is one that can fly almost straight overhead. A kite that gets up only to a 30- or 40-degree point in the sky is considered a failure. There have also been many kite fights over East Hampton's beaches—fights without glassed lines or razor-blade-carrying kites, but simply Tomi Ungerer and another kiteflyer, each maneuvering his flying charge in an attempt to get beneath the other and then drive upward into the understructure of the opposing kite.

Tomi Ungerer's kites have often confused bathers on the long rolling stretches of sand. With wet algae hanging from the string, the kite slips down over a dozing sunbather until the algae sweeps across the bather's back. Then, with a pull of the string, the kite is sent shooting straight up into the air leaving a bewildered vacationer trying to figure out what has happened.

But whether it is a solitary kite flying in the damp blue-gray fog that rolls in off the Atlantic, or thirty of Ungerer's creations flying together in the sky from different points on the same line, his focus is on experiments and building. And although the joy is great, a certain frustration is inherent in the kites. For, to Tomi Ungerer, as to most who design and build their own kites, occasionally after completing a flying form that "has" to be unique, the discovery is made by watching other kites or glancing at an old book, that someone in Thailand or New Zealand or India or France or the United States made basically the same kite sometime between 1000 B.C. and 1910. But the next one—nobody could have made it.

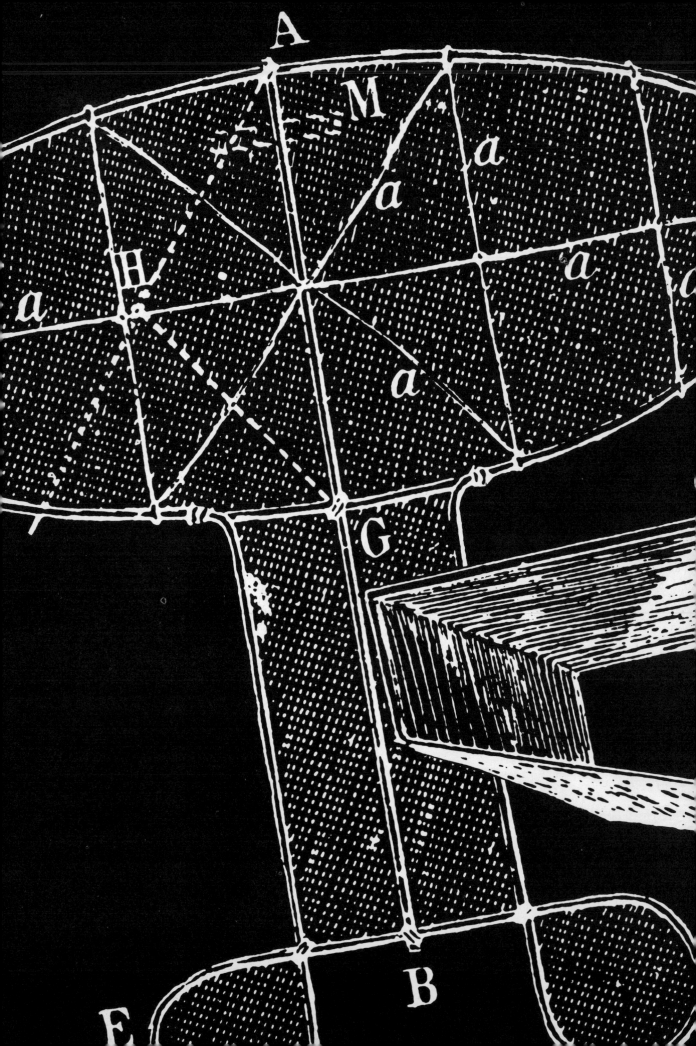

Celebrating the resumption of kiteflying contests in Japan in 1947, this giant—weighing, with string, 1,440 pounds—was launched in Hoojubana, Jap

# Some Highlights

◆ A flurry of kiteflying activity by women in Columbus, Ohio, in the spring of 1949 was as important in terms of the sport as what was going on in China in the second century B.C. March 21 was a big day for Mrs. Doris Acosta, for on that day she broke her own housewife kiteflying record, having kept her ten-cent kite aloft, almost out of sight, at the end of 5,100 feet of string. Only five days earlier she had set an endurance record of twenty-three and a half hours and celebrated it by announcing that she would return and break her initial record by keeping a kite up until Easter (seventeen days) if she could. An unexpected spring snowstorm knocked her second record-breaking kite down at the end of its twenty-ninth hour. Mrs. Acosta's effort was consistent with kite history in that it took only three days for another Columbus housewife, Mrs. Harry King, to attempt to top the mark. On March 25, thirty-eight hours after Mrs. King's kite was put up, it fell down, and the world had a new housewife kiteflying champion.

Kite records and attempts to utilize kites "efficiently" are, almost entirely, a product of the Western world. People who have always lived with kites, the Chinese, Japanese, Koreans, Tonkinese, Thais, and Indians, have been more or less content to stay close to the basic emotions and aesthetics that result from kiteflying as a form of joy and art. But as early as the eighteenth century Westerners were determined to find a function for kites.

Mrs. Harry King and her children during her "record-setting" kite flight in Columbus, Ohio

Benjamin Franklin's "Memorable Experiment with the Kite"

In 1754, before there were any legal Americans, Benjamin Franklin became the American of record to introduce the kite to science. Franklin's writings retell his famous electrical experiment:

"Make a small cross of two light strips of cedar, the arms so long as to reach to the four corners of a large thin silk handkerchief to the extremities of the cross, so you have the body of a kite, which being properly accommodated with a tail, loop and string will rise in the air, like those made of paper; but this being of silk is fitter to bear the wet and wind of a thundergust without tearing. To the top of the upright stick of the cross is to be fixed a very sharp pointed wire, rising a foot or more above the wood. To the end of the twine, next to the hand is to be tied a silk ribbon, and where the silk and twine join, a key may be fastened. This kite is to be raised when a thunder-gust appears to be coming on, and the person who holds the string must stand within a door or window or under some cover, so the silk ribbon may not become wet; and care must be taken that twine does not touch the frame of the door or the window."

Franklin's chronic curiosity and inventiveness gave him a minor shock and proof that lightning is electrical. A year later a Russian professor tried to duplicate the experiment and was permanently dispatched by a thunderbolt. And as recently as the early 1960s the United States Department of Defense reconfirmed the difficulty of Dr. Franklin's experiment. After two years of attempts with

Lawrence Hargrave, inventor of the box kite, photographed in 1896

A Hargrave box kite with multiple cells

Early Hargrave kite with rectangular cells connected with a single boom

Modified Hargrave box kite, used in the Blue Hill Station weather experiments

kites, and then balloons, to make lightning strike, an official thunderstorm study group in New Mexico succeeded by arming themselves with giant bows and arrows and firing fine wires high into lightning-charged clouds.

Franklin took kites into the world of science and commerce, and in the years since his experiment the skies of France, England, Germany, Italy, and the United States have been filled with kites on very distinct missions. The men who followed Franklin's lead adapted kites into meteorology, photography, lifesaving, signaling, war, telegraphy, and as a link in the search for engine-powered flight. Without exception these efforts, whether or not successful, have been repeated with minor variations up to the present.

One of the major additions to kiteflying came nearly three thousand years after the first kite was flown somewhere in Asia. In the 1870s Lawrence Hargrave, an Australian naturalist and inventor, became deeply involved in an attempt to create a successful airplane structure. Through his experiments he developed a number of cellular kites and what has come to be known as the basic box kite. And the box kite made an immediate and major impact within the field of scientific kiteflying. The box's stability and lifting power as a wind-held kite were what made possible most of the air experiments of the precedent-shattering years between 1885 and 1910. It was a variation of Hargrave's basic box form that was flown as the first airplane by the Wright brothers. It was a combination

Flying a modified Hargrave box kite at the Blue Hill Station

Modified Hargrave kite with a meteorograph attached to the frame

of a Hargrave box kite and Benjamin Franklin's "antenna" that was flown by Marconi in Nova Scotia when he drew in the first transatlantic radio signal in 1901. The Hargrave box kite also served as the workhorse of the meteorological experiments carried on by the United States Weather Bureau at the Blue Hill Station in Massachusetts, beginning in 1894. The Weather Bureau kites carried meteorographs for the testing of temperature, wind velocity, and humidity at increasing altitudes.

By 1899 the Weather Bureau's kiting systems (box kites attached to a main line at two-thousand-foot intervals) had developed to a point where the measuring equipment was consistently lifted to altitudes exceeding 10,000 feet. The land power to control the powerful kite system was provided after 1896 by a sturdy steam-driven windlass, a modification of an apparatus developed by Sir William Thompson for deep-sea sounding. The windlass' reel could hold up to 40,000 feet of 14-gauge (0.03 inch) wire, which was spliced together at 8,000-foot intervals. The scientists at Blue Hill turned to kites after becoming disillusioned with balloons. As was typical of the dialogue between science kiters and science balloonists, the choice was justified in definite terms. "Compared with balloons, kites are much less expensive, more easily handled, and the exposure of the instrument [the meterographs] is probably equal to that of the instruments at the ground . . . something impossible to obtain with instruments carried by balloons. Another great advantage is that the kites are controllable and the records may be obtained at any desired point up to over 12,000 feet. While the heights reached heretofore do not equal the highest balloon ascensions, the progress made so far warrants the belief that a height of three miles is possible."

The three-mile height not only proved to be possible but was ultimately doubled by the Weather Bureau. In 1931, with a system not unlike that employed in the early Blue Hill experiments, the Bureau put a series of eight kites up on a wire line to an altitude of 31,955 feet—an altitude record that continues to stand. The Weather Bureau closed down its last kite station in 1933 and went back to work with greatly improved balloons.

Steam-powered kite-winding machine used during the Blue Hill experiments

Modified Hargrave Blue Hill kite

Shortly before the Blue Hill experiments, William Eddy, a photographer from Bayonne, New Jersey, became one of the few Western kiteflyers who continue to stand in a class with Lawrence Hargrave. Three years before Hargrave's development of the box kite, Eddy received credit for introducing a modified Malay two-stick kite to the Western world. The traditional Malay kite and the many variations of that early form required sizable tails in order to fly with a degree of steadiness in moderate to heavy winds. In most of its forms the cross stick was considerably shorter than the height of the kite, and both sticks rested flat against the fabric cover. Eddy's innovation was to make the dimensions nearly equal and to bow the cross stick. It worked, and, in the years since, the modified Eddy has become the world's most popular pleasure kite.

Eddy also gained considerable fame as a kite photographer; yet although he became the most famous man to suspend cameras from kites, he was not the first. This "first" was credited in 1887 to E. D. Archibald, an English scientist who gained notice during his lifetime for his early meteorological studies. Archibald was only a few months ahead of Arthur Batut, a French kite experimenter who began hanging cameras from kites early in 1888 and triggered the shutter with a simple explosive device set off by a long-burning fuse. Eddy described his early work in 1897 in an article published in *The Century* magazine. He prefaced his report by claiming to have taken "the first aerial kite photograph of any kind taken in the Western Hemisphere." His early photographs often contained portions of the kite, but he soon overcame the problem by developing a triangular stick frame that attached to the main kite-line so the camera could expose itself to a relatively horizontal view. He also became aware of the inherent "risks" of his photo system.

"It was imperative that I should send up and draw in the camera as rapidly as possible. The chief danger in mid-air kite photography is that the strong pull of forty or fifty pounds used to lift the camera may break the line. This strain may be more than tripled any moment by a gust. While I was photographing the great Sound Money Parade of October, 1896, with a camera suspended above Broad-

(top) Diagrammatic drawings for patent papers for William Eddy's kite

(middle) Photographer Arthur Batut's first aerial photographic system

(bottom) Facsimile of a Batut photograph taken at an altitude of 127 meters by his kite-suspended camera

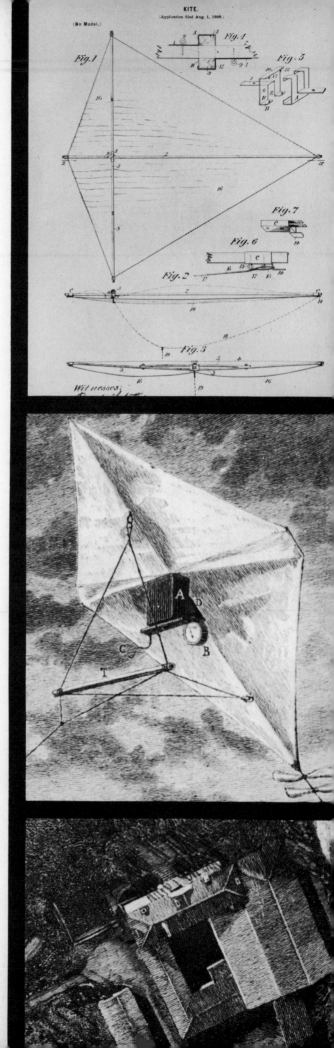

way in New York, the main kite cable was broken in a peculiar way. Three kites built for light winds were at a great height when they were borned down by a gust, the main kite-line becoming entangled in the high iron framework of an unfinished structure on the east side of Broadway, the kites having been sent up from the roof at the corner of Broadway and Duane Street. The main cable was snapped by an attempt to drag in the entangled line, the three kites and one flag disappearing to the eastward. They were never recovered. Meantime the camera fell with a swinging motion to the top of the next building, far below the level of the fourteen-story building from which I had sent out the line of kites. I was obliged to crawl across the wire netting in an interior court before I recovered the camera and replaced it in the line. I then continued my mid-air photographing until nearly 5 p.m. . . ."

Eddy worked closely with most of America's early scientific kiteflyers and in 1895 spent some time with J. Woodbrige Davis. Davis had already gained a degree of fame as a developer of a kite apparatus for use in assisting stranded shipping passengers to the shore from foundering vessels. The French magazine *La Nature* described the system in 1892:

"As soon as the kite is raised and the guy lines are adjusted so that it is directed aright, these [guy lines] are secured to a wooden float or buoy and the latter is thrown overboard having fast to it a light but strong line which is paid out as the kite flies to the land dragging the buoy through the water. When the float reaches the beach the lifesaving crew detaches it, and fastens it to the ship's rope, the regular lines and blocks which the wrecked seamen then haul out to their vessel and make secure according to the directions found painted on the small wooden tags fastened to the blocks. The crew is then brought to land either in the breeches-buoy or life-car hauled out to them by the lifesaving crew."

Together, Eddy and Davis successfully demonstrated a method of sending messages ashore from ships. Davis' buoys towed by Eddy's kites effectively made it across the Kill van Kull between New Jersey and Staten Island.

(top) William Eddy's kite-suspended aerial camera

(middle) Elements of Woodbridge Davis' lifesaving kite system

(bottom) A distress signal being sent to shore by a Davis kite

Maillot's giant kite lifting a weight of seventy kilograms

The framework of "Uncle Sam's" large kite

The completed kite bearing "Uncle Sam's" crest

In the midst of the nineteenth-century activity, the giant kites began making their appearances in Western skies. The giants were constructed and flown primarily for science but on occasion were put up for the sheer excitement of making and flying something big.

The ancient dream of manned flight had caused a number of men, such as Hargrave, to turn to kites. In 1883 one of the most remarkable kites ever constructed was unveiled by the French inventor Marcel Maillot. His octagonal kite measured 32 feet across and had an over-all sail surface of 775 square feet. Its first experimental use took place in May, 1886, when it lifted a 150-pound bag of ballast to a height 30 feet above the ground. After months of experiments and improvements in its intricate landline system the kite proved capable of sustaining a maximum weight of 594 pounds. Whether to carry men or simply to take up considerable space in the sky, the big kites proved to be a fascination, and on August 31, 1892, an American claimed the world big kite record. The flyer never identified himself publicly by any name other than Uncle Sam, and his crew caused a considerable stir, both at its flying site, Dudley Hill, Massachusetts, and in Paris. La Nature, in reporting the flight, challenged both Uncle Sam's attitude and the truth of the record claim: "When asked why such a big kite, the explanation was very American. A kite of eleven feet in height had been launched a few months earlier in nearby Salem, Massachusetts, and Uncle Sam desired to surpass it as the biggest kite in the world."

The publication, although impressed with the fact that Uncle Sam's kite was planned, constructed, and flown in only sixteen days, set the record straight for its readers: "We remind the Americans that it was on this side of the ocean that the first giant kites were constructed, and that M. Maillot's kite, capable of carrying a man, was constructed quite some time ago. However, we salute these amateurs who have occupied their time well. Their experimental kite offers perhaps some useful applications."

"Uncle Sam" at the kite line

Members of the kiteflying team

Alphonso Woodall ready for an overland kite ride

(top right) Woodall riding high over Cleveland, Ohio

One interesting "application" was witnessed sixty-seven years later in southern California. During the 1950s Alphonso Woodall, then of Cleveland, Ohio, achieved considerable recognition as a great kite-rider. Unlike most modern kite-riders who are towed only over water behind power boats, Woodall was willing to float at the end of a line over land. He did have some overwater experience, however, and in 1957 was towed across Lake Erie from Cleveland, hanging from his six-sided fourteen-foot kite. That same year he began planning for an English Channel kite crossing to take place in late 1959.

The television program *You Asked for It* enjoyed wide popularity in the late fifties spotlighting unusual hobbies and talents "asked for" by the nation's viewers. Alphonso Woodall "asked for it" regarding his own kite-riding. A few weeks later he was on an airport runway at Sun Valley, California, tightly lacing his boots which were firmly connected to water skis which rested upon roller skates. After being strapped into his large and often-ridden kite, he took a firm grasp on a towline fed out to him from a reel attached to the back of a car. Television cameras were in position, and all waited for the director's signal. A production assistant held a lettered board in front of the main camera for a few seconds. "Woodall, the Kite-Rider, Take One." The car accelerated smoothly, and Woodall and his kite coasted down the runway and slowly began to lift skyward. Within seconds Alphonso Woodall was riding through the air fifty feet above the tarmac runway. The *You Asked for It* audience never saw the flight on their television sets. For at the fifty-foot altitude the kite, whacked by a crosscurrent, lost its wind.

Woodall's *You Asked for It* flight at Sun Valley, California

Alphonso Woodall and his kite plummeted to the runway's surface and instead of a few moments of national television, Woodall had a broken leg and two broken heels. In spite of this experience Woodall was back on snow skis within a year, and two years after what could have been a fatal accident, he successfully "rode" his kite for the Mike Douglas television show, landing smoothly and triumphantly.

Alphonso Woodall never made his English Channel attempt, but in the early 1960s a number of adventuresome Frenchmen took part in a flurry of channel flights. The first men to make the difficult air voyage were Gil Delamare and Jean-Claude Dubois, towed on individual kites from Calais to Dover, England, on October 17, 1962. Dubois had the most involved launching and the fastest flight time. With his eighteen-foot kite strapped across his shoulders he ran along the Calais beach for one hundred yards as his towboat gathered speed. He was then swept to an altitude of three hundred feet and was pulled across the channel at a speed of seventeen miles per hour. Dubois' crossing took only 74 minutes— 21 minutes faster than M. Delamare's. Two weeks later the men again made the trip. The second flight from France to England was capped off, after an hour's rest on the English seashore, by a kite ride back to Calais.

Two years later 37-year-old French kiteman Bernard Danis brought out his unique kite and, wearing a rubber suit and water skis, completed the Calais-to-Dover journey in 101 minutes. Although this was somewhat slower than the crossings made by Delamare and Dubois, it was the fastest time on "record" for any water-ski-wearing channel kiteflyer.

French kite-rider Bernard Danis swooping toward Dover, England, and the completion of his Channel crossing

Although not seeking records, two American inventors have, in recent years, made a major impact on recreational and scientific kiteflying. Dr. Francis Rogallo unveiled his kite, the Flexi-Wing, in New York City in 1943. The Flexi-Wing, an air foil that assumes different shapes depending upon changes in wind velocity, was developed after years of testing and has become a familiar form to sport flyers and space scientists. Rogallo, who has had major responsibilities in the United States space program since the founding of the National Aeronautics and Space Administration, has continued to create designs that have been adapted to advanced test forms as space vehicle reentry parachutes as well as a number of other NASA applications.

Domina Jalbert, a gentle and determined man, has also had his inventions accepted for both play and science. Jalbert, considered by many of the "major" kite flyers as the outstanding kiteman in the United States, began flying kites as a child in Canada, and as a young man in the late 1930s constructed and flew kites that carried advertising banners over Woonsocket, Rhode Island. At the outbreak of World War II he was working as a rigger for a construction company. It was the war that made "things that flew" more than a hobby. He went to work for the U. S. Rubber Company as a military balloon rigger and began his kite and flight experiments in earnest. By the end of the war the Jalbert Kitoon, a combination kite and balloon, was being widely used by the military. His more standard kites were also causing a considerable stir throughout New England's scientific community. In 1943, to demonstrate the power that could be gained through properly controlled kites, he launched his then twelve-year-old daughter on one of his giant kites. His basic approach to engineless flight is simply that the wind, a force that can be destructive, should be made to work for men.

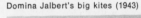

Dr. Francis Rogallo flying one of his first nonrigid Para-Foils (1943)

Domina Jalbert's big kites (1943)

Throughout his career his focus has been on harnessing the wind to do what he wanted. His kites and balloons were put to work in the forties by Massachusetts Institute of Technology researchers and were used extensively by the Woods Hole Oceanographic Institute. The Woods Hole experimenters used the kites to suspend sonar equipment in order to make ocean depth soundings.

In the years immediately after the war Jalbert worked on balloons for the Dewey and Almy Chemical Co. Balloons, in Jalbert's words, "expensive, cumbersome, fickle with no two alike," had limited effectiveness in anything other than ideal moderate wind conditions. Jalbert turned back to the big kites. Again he met with limitations, for after six to eight hours of constant flying, the sticks would bend out of shape, and if sticks strong enough to hold shape were used, the kite weight became prohibitive. He threw away the sticks and began working on parachutes.

He began the final stage of his breakthrough in 1953 while visiting Patrick Air Force Base with a skydiving team which he was sponsoring. Watching an airplane glide into a landing, his thoughts came together. He measured the plane's wings and began the design and construction of a nonrigid fabric wing. Within months he had the Jalbert Air-Foil, an amalgam of the positive attributes of balloons, kites, and parachutes, and combined it with a barrage balloon suspension system. The Jalbert Air-Foil, operating on ram-air principles, proved to be a highly dependable "kite" and has served scientists throughout the world efficiently and consistently.

Jalbert's sense of vision and innovation has continued. In 1968 he demonstrated the Jalbert Para-Sled, an advanced statement of his research. The sled, taking advantage of the wind's tremendous power, opens up at the shock of being struck by the wind's force and

A seventeen-foot Jalbert kite taking to the air

Jalbert's kite winch with 1,500 feet on one-half-inch manila line

uses the available wind to inflate itself. Once inflated it holds its shape, and if it ultimately lands on water, it becomes its own raft. Its varied and important uses are being investigated within the United States space program. Through the years Jalbert's kites and balloons and, most importantly, his knowledge and insight have been used by the University of London, Hamburg University, Sweden's Upsala University, the United States Department of Defense, and many imaginative kite flyers. Domina Jalbert, operating the Jalbert Space Laboratory in Boca Raton, Florida, maintains a steady view concerning his kites. "Let's face it. We don't fly kites. They fly themselves. All we can do is try to control them."

Jim Moran, one of America's greatest public relations men, was arrested in 1951 for trying to control a nonrigid kite. Moran, who gained legendary status as the man who sold a refrigerator to an Eskimo, found a needle in a haystack, hatched an ostrich egg, and

A Jalbert Air-Foil climbing into the air (1968)

arranged for a client's dog to receive "the bone to the city of New York," had his brush with kiteflying fame in Central Park. He has always been a kiteflyer, and when one of his clients, a candy manufacturer, faced the problem of promoting a candy bar, Moran's thoughts turned to kites. He announced to the public that he had formed the Moran Midget Employment Stabilization Board and that, using the potential of the board he would unveil an entirely new concept of advertising on a Saturday morning in Central Park. The Stabilization Board was to address itself to the difficult problem of assuring year-round employment to midgets, a group which in Moran's mind, had difficulty finding anything other than seasonal circus work.

With the aid of kiteflying friends he built a large, twelve-foot-wide nonrigid kite based on Dr. Rogallo's designs. With three midgets, none weighing more than sixty-five pounds, he made his way into New Jersey for a test flight. The kite flew well and, using a block and tackle, he hoisted two of the midgets up on the kite's line. The major problem encountered by the midgets was that their "chairs" spun around out of control. In Moran's words, "A spinning midget is an unhappy midget." He had some small rudders constructed and attached them to the midgets' waists.

A few days later Jim Moran, three midgets, a ground crew made up of friends in the communications business, and a number of radio, television, and newspaper reporters convened in the Park Meadow. Moran explained his new advertising medium. The midgets, dressed in costumes and armed with megaphones, were to be floated up into the air by the kite and then moved past apartment-house windows. The rudder-wearing midgets were instructed that if anyone looked out of a window and saw them, they were to put the megaphones to their mouths and bellow, "Buy Our Candy Bars!" As the head of Midget Employment Stabilization Board and his ground crew prepared to launch the kite, a policeman walked up to the group and announced, "You can't fly no midgets from no kites." Moran, a man who likes to know all of the details, asked to see the city ordinance against flying midgets from kites. After a few minutes of heated conversation the police officer pointed to a nearby baseball game and explained why Moran had to be arrested. "If one of your midgets fell, he could hurt a ballplayer." Moran was marched off to the Nineteenth Precinct Police Station, and the Moran Midget Employment Stabilization Board ceased its operations.

Jim Moran, a kiteflyer

Jim Moran, wearing highland cap, being led to the Nineteenth Precinct Station, with his "riders" and kite crew

An unidentified, early kite passenger

# Fighters and Floaters

◆ A kite, even an Indian fighting kite, is by its nature a peaceful and reflective object. Yet throughout the history of warfare men have attempted to adapt kites to the particular needs of battle.

Kites have been taken into battle since the second century B.C. when a Chinese general, Han Sin, is said to have used kites for signaling and in making military engineering measurements. Records also state that early Korean and Japanese military leaders used man-carrying kites for observation purposes. As more modern men have learned to create sophisticated weapons for defensive and offensive military use, attempts have been made to continue development of a number of kite forms. The French Army first made use of kites as signaling aids in the 1890s. The British military machine of the same period had one of history's most dedicated kiteflyers attempting to convince his commanders of the value of using man-carrying kites. Engine-powered

flight was still several years in the future when Captain Baden Baden-Powell, the younger brother of the founder of the Boy Scouts, financed and supervised his own experiments. His tandem-kite suspension system, with a complex system of ground anchors and a swinging observation bucket, stayed aloft more often than it fell. In *The World* magazine in 1896 Baden-Powell put forth his strongest plea for his work. After discussing the negative aspects of balloon-suspended observers, he described his work with his kites.

"My thoughts soon turned to that simple toy, the kite. Thus the wind, which is so detrimental to ballooning now became my helpmate. Yet, let me at once explain I do not consider it an absolute necessity. As a schoolboy runs to get his kite to rise, so this aerial apparatus may be towed by running men or horses, and so caused to ascend in calm weather. The latest machine consists of a varying number (usually four to six) of sails, of a flattened hexagonal shape, looking not unlike the square sails of a ship. These are connected one behind the other to the ground line, from which latter is suspended a basket car. A parachute is spread out above the car in case of accident. The number of kites used depends upon the strength of the wind, and thus, the stronger the pressure the less is the area presented so that the strain on the retaining ropes is always the same.

"This apparatus has now been tried on a number of occasions and under many different circumstances of weather. And although through lack of wind, or rather insufficiency of kite-power, it has occasionally not lifted as well as I should have liked, and frequent mishaps, the results of inexperience have occurred, yet on the whole it has behaved very well, and has generally carried its man easily and steadily to a considerable height. I have myself been lifted over a hundred feet high, and had I not been firmly held down by a rope I might have risen much higher. Never once have I experienced the least uncomfortable motion. When the car has been let up to the full extent of the rope, equivalent to a height of some four hundred feet, it has invariably floated steadily and well."

The problem in getting a new system

Baden Baden-Powell demonstrates his kite-suspended observer system (1896)

accepted was then, as now, related directly to money. The captain met this situation head on.

"It is a pity that in this so-called miserable life of ours we have always to consider that wretched question of filthy lucre. It is one which ought to have no place in the minds of soldiers, at all events, when purchasing their outfit. But unfortunately a soldier is but a servant and slave of that mean, tight-fisted gentleman, the tax-payer, and his even more miserly representative, the Treasury. New inventions are often brought forward which, if adopted, might add greatly to the efficiency of the army. But the wherewithal to acquire the necessary article is generally wanting. So we must see whether supposing this air-car should prove to be an efficient acquisition to our powers of offense and defense, we can, as a nation, afford to adopt. Let us consider the necessary outlay. I am unable to give any exact figures as to the cost of the machine, as my own hours of labor would be one of the chief items. Nevertheless, I say that I believe a complete machine could be made at a government yard for about five pounds. The cost of maintenance would be but a trifle. It may be mentioned that our present balloon establishment costs us about three thousand pounds a year. Can we, then, as one of the leading powers of Europe afford say twenty pounds to thoroughly investigate and completely put to the test this, as I think, promising invention, bearing in mind that it is possible that by its adoption we may be saved spending the three thousand pounds a year on balloons?"

The British Army withheld its official sanction, but Baden-Powell was not finished with his work. During the Boer War the captain volunteered for assignment to the battle lines and left his kites at home in England. The fighting between long trenches was such that the side gaining an observation advantage of even twenty feet above the ground could have a tremendous advantage; thus Baden-Powell's commander asked if he could construct a kite observation platform. The kite, however, never saw battle, for as work was being completed on the structure, the war ended.

The years of Baden-Powell's experiments saw a number of men working on virtually identical military observation systems.

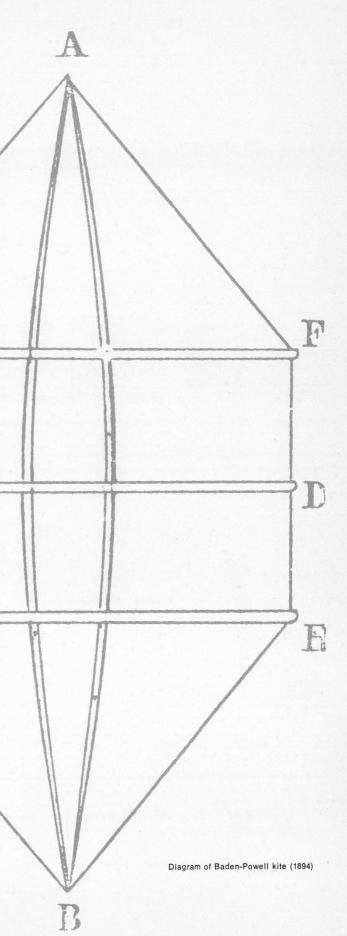

Diagram of Baden-Powell kite (1894)

Lieutenant Hugh D. Wise (1896)

It was in this period that Lieutenant Hugh D. Wise of the United States Army Signal Corps began his efforts. The idea of using kites as supports for signal apparatus was suggested to Lieutenant Wise by his commanding officer, Captain James Allen, at Governors Island, New York, in 1896. At Allen's urging, Wise became deeply involved in the subject and within months was one of the world's leading kite experts. Two soldier-assistants were assigned to his experiments, and the three men began constructing kites and flying them daily over New York's busy harbor from the island parade grounds. At the beginning the young lieutenant was aware of a lack of popular acceptance: "I was generally regarded as a candidate for the Army insane asylum and certainly, had I been playing marbles in the street with my assistants we should have received no more pitying glances from passers-by." The results came quickly, however, and within a few months systems of signal flags, semaphores, lanterns, and flares suspended from the kites and controlled by ground cords were successfully demonstrated.

The signaling experiments depleted the small budget that Captain Allen had been able to scrape together for the kites. Lieutenant Wise soon received an offer from the New York *Tribune* to construct and fly kites with banners displaying the results of the upcoming 1896 presidential election. The newspaper commissioned the construction of the necessary kites. The banners carrying the news of McKinley's election and, following this announcement, a huge American flag, flew a few thousand feet over the newspaper's tower in lower Manhattan. The profits from the project and some money received for a number of magazine articles provided the lieutenant with enough money to continue his signaling experiments and to begin working toward man-carrying observer kites. The initial observer

A chemical-light signal

Twelve-foot Eddy kite
used in Wise experiments

Sending signals via kites

Displaying the flag over lower Broadway, New York City

test took the form of a four-kite "tandem" from which a 150-pound dummy called "Jimmy" was suspended at an altitude of 200 feet over New York's harbor. The following day the flight was again attempted, but because of a fouling of the line, the stuffed rider plunged to the ground. Writing in *The Century* magazine, Lieutenant Wise described the work that followed "Jimmy's" mixed successes:

"A day or two after the experiment with the dummy an incident occurred which, though ridiculous well nigh resulted seriously. The same kites that bore the dummy aloft had been sent up about two hundred feet, when the two men who were assisting me went for another kite, leaving me alone at the windlass. Noticing that the rope was in danger of being cut by the cogs I put on the brake and passing around to the front, bore down on the rope. In order to readjust the rope on the drum it was necessary to relieve the tension. Near the windlass a piece of rope had been spliced to the main line as a leader for the cord of another kite. This I wrapped around my waist and tied with a bow; then, drawing my knife, I cut the main line from the windlass. I was not long in discovering my mistake, for as the rope parted the knife flew from my hand, I was jerked over on my back, and started for a sleigh ride across the grass at a rapid pace. In my efforts to untie the bow I pulled the wrong end and made a hard knot. Finally I managed to get to my feet; but this was little better and in spite of my efforts I was rapidly approaching the seawall. . . . A friendly lamp-post happened to be directly in the line of travel. I approached it with outstretched arms, clasped it in a fond embrace, and there I hung until assistance arrived."

A few days after this near-serious accident occurred, Hugh D. Wise made his first kite-riding attempt, as reported in *The Century*:

"On an afternoon when the anemometer showed a wind-velocity of twenty-two miles an hour [four] kites with a combined lifting surface of two hundred and two square feet were taken out. Eight hundred feet of 7/16th inch manila rope was run out and stretched to leeward, and to it, a kite was made fast. Sixty feet of rope capable of a strain of seven hundred and fifty pounds was tied to the back of the first kite and stretched in prolongation of the other rope and to its end kite B was made fast. A man was stationed by each kite to hold it flat upon the ground. A pulley was lashed to the main line close up to kite D, and over it passed a long rope to one end of which a boatswain's chair was attached, my idea being to allow the kites to rise unhampered at first, and when they became steady to hoist myself to them, then to cleat the halyard to the chair and allow the kites to rise.

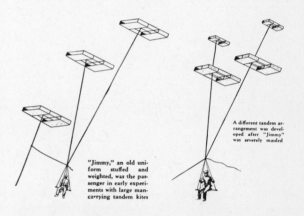

"Jimmy," an old uniform stuffed and weighted, was the passenger in early experiments with large man-carrying tandem kites

A different tandem arrangement was developed after "Jimmy" was severely mauled

Launching a large kite from Governors Island

"Taking my seat in the chair I gave the signal. The man at B raised its front edge, and it bounded into the air followed by D, and the halyard spun over the pulley. Anticipating a jerk on the main line I had stationed six men to hold it in front of the windlass in order to lessen the jar upon the kites. I had underestimated, however, the tremendous power of the tandem; for as it rose the men were dragged forward and the rope tightened upon the windlass with a jerk that tore the central truss from the lower kite. The two upper kites, steadied by the weight of the helpless lower one, floated away. As they passed over the fort they were caught by some soldiers, and the tandem was saved, though the kites were broken against the neighboring walls. So ended this experiment and the work of weeks had been torn to pieces in a few moments."

The abrupt end of Lieutenant Wise's first kite-riding attempt

During the next two months Wise and his men repaired the broken kites and constructed the largest Hargrave-type kite ever built to that time. On January 22, 1897, at 4 p.m. with a fifteen-mile-per-hour wind blowing across Governors Island, the lieutenant began his second attempt at kite-riding, again described in *The Century*:

"As I had more power than I needed, I decided to send up two tandems, and to unite them, since this greatly facilitated their management. The windlass, wound with five hundred feet of 1/2-inch rope was placed in position and lashed to a tree. C was launched and tied to the back of B, and the two kites were allowed to rise to the end of one hundred and fifty feet of rope, which was made fast to a tree. One hundred feet of rope was now run from the windlass and made fast to E, to the back of which F, having been launched was tied. Six men took hold of the rope fifty feet from E, the man stationed by the kite raised its front edge, and it rose gracefully from the ground. The strain was given gradually to the windlass, and then the first tandem was brought up and tied to the main line. At the point of junction the same apparatus used in

the last experiment was made fast and the kites were allowed to rise until the pulley was about thirty feet from the ground, when taking my seat in the chair, I was hoisted to the pulley. The line sagged badly, so that I was at a height of only about twenty feet. In a few minutes the breeze died out considerably, and I was lowered to the ground where I waited for the wind to freshen.

"After a short wait the wind rose to seventeen miles an hour, and when I was hoisted to the pulley there was not a great sag in the line. I made the halyard fast to the chair, and gave the signal to the men. As the rope ran out the kites bore me up until I was as high as the neighboring houses, a measurement showed a height of forty-two feet from the ground to the chair. The sensation was not at all unpleasant . . . a gentle swaying and lifting not unlike the motion of a swing. I was tempted to go higher for there would have been no difficulty; but I was not provided with a parachute, and I did not wish to run any unnecessary risk. After remaining aloft a short while and observing the action of the kites, I signaled to wind in, and when near the ground I was lowered by the pulley with

the satisfaction of knowing that this experiment at least had been a success, and that it was the first kite ascension in the United States."

Lieutenant Wise's kite work led him into the field of gliders, and during the months that followed his successful kite ride, he developed and flew a number of "gliding machines." In the spring of 1898 he was assigned, with his regiment, to Florida for mobilization in the Spanish-American War. The glider experiments ended, but his work with kites was not over. The main Spanish fleet led by Admiral Cervera was menacing the American transports going to and from Cuba. The location of Cervera's flagship was not known, although it was thought to be in the harbor at Santiago. It was proposed that Lieutenant Wise's kites be put up beyond the harbor's mouth and aerial photographs taken of the harbor's interior. The system was successfully tested near the mobilization center at Tampa, Florida. But, as was the case with Baden-Powell and his kites in the Boer War, the need vanished. Cervera's presence was confirmed before Wise was able to put his kites into action.

World War I kite-supported observer systems

Although both Hugh Wise and Baden Baden-Powell began working in other areas of flight, their basic observer systems, with minor changes, were incorporated into the service of the French, Germans, British, and the Americans. All of the major combatants involved in World War I made limited use of kite-riding observers, but the introduction of armed airplanes precluded any wide-ranging values.

The United States Army had adopted two man-carrying kites, one a twelve-foot-high Eddy-style kite for use in low winds, and the second, a nine-to-twelve-foot-high winged box kite for flying in moderate and heavy winds. The individual kite-rider's vulnerability was acknowledged but not solved. One suggestion for protection was to give the rider his own weapons with which to repel airplane attacks.

It was thought that small captive balloons attached to the observer's belt, and having a high explosive concentrated in bombs under the balloons, could be used to combat hostile airplanes. The explosions of these bombs were to be actuated by an electric current, controlled by buttons located on the observer's belt. The observer was also to be able to communicate with the earth through a telephone with a transmitter attached to his chest and receivers fastened over his ears. Thus it would not be necessary for the observer to descend to transmit information regarding gun range, the movement of enemy troops, or the location of enemy artillery. It can be assumed that a critic pointed out what could happen if an individual blew a bomb off over his head. The proposal was not implemented.

"This aerial scout makes observations and communicates with his base below by telephone while he is protected by floating bombs which he can explode upon enemy aircraft"

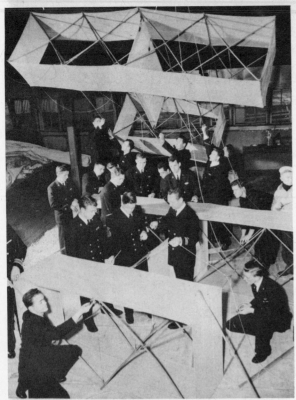

Kiteflying training at the U. S. Barrage Balloon and Kite School

Launching a barrage kite from a ship's deck

World War II, with the many "sophisticated" weapons developed through broader industrialization, still made use of the kite. The United States Maritime Barrage Balloon and Kite School was opened in New York City. Giant airplane-shaped box kites were constructed and their uses taught to men. The kites (unmanned) were put up from ships, in place of barrage balloons, making it difficult for enemy aircraft to sweep in low.

Most of the military kite work of the twentieth century has been done with typical military anonymity. Paul Garber of the National Air Museum, however, gained considerable notice for his efforts. On the morning of December 8, 1941, Garber, then curator of air science for the Smithsonian Institution, with a broad background and experience in all phases of aeronautics, volunteered for navy duty. He received a direct commission as a lieutenant commander assigned to the Special Services Division of the Navy's Bureau of Aeronautics in Washington, D.C. Paul Garber found himself committed to aerology when, as a small boy in Columbus, Ohio, he watched Wilbur and Orville Wright demonstrate their flying machine. Although an expert in all forms of the subject, he has always had a special fondness for kites and kiteflying. His opportunity to make use of his specialized knowledge came in 1943 when he heard Admiral John H. Towers state that the navy needed an improved moving target to speed up the training of aircraft gunners.

At the time Garber was involved in the production of model airplanes used by the military for instruction in aircraft recognition. But he wondered if perhaps a kite could solve the problem brought up by the admiral. Working during evenings with the help of two friends and fellow kite buffs, Lloyd Reichert and Stanley Potter, it took Paul Garber less than a year to solve the problem. He developed a kite that could simulate nearly every maneuver of an airplane. This was accomplished by adding a keel and a rudder to a basic two-stick kite and controlling it with twin flying lines fed out from a double-drum wooden reel with hand brakes. When he felt that he had effectively mastered the problem, he scheduled a demonstration for Captain Luis de Florez, chief of the Special Services Division. Garber put his kite through a spectacular series of loops, zigs, dives, and figure eights. He then capped the session by moving the kite through a script-style signature of "L-u-i-s d-e F-l-o-r-e-z" and then swiftly swept the kite back to the left and dotted the "i." More than 100,000 of the kites were used by both the navy and army prior to the end of the war.

Flying Paul Garber's seven-foot target kites at the Naval Air Station, Anacostia, 1944

One of the most ambitious attempts to adapt kites to warfare was made by the German Navy in the latter stages of World War II. In late 1943 an intricate, collapsible, man-lifting autogiro kite, consisting of an observer's chair to which a lifting rotor was attached, was tested over the Bay of Danzig. There were rumors that a number of men fell during the initial sequence of tests, but by the spring of 1944 the kite was put into limited operational use by the German U-boat fleet. The giro kites, under a shroud of secrecy, were assigned as observer equipment to Monsun IX-d-2 submarines for use in East Asian waters. The kite, stowed below deck, was to be brought up and unfolded on the sub's afterdeck. The submarine would then turn against the wind with full power, the rotor prop would begin spinning in the wind, and the observer-passenger, armed with binoculars, could be lifted into the air at the end of a cable carrying a telephone line. The submarine, cruising into the wind, served as a supplement to the air's lifting power and, with the broadened horizon that was viewed from an altitude of two to three hundred feet, the sub, in theory, was to be more efficient in picking out shipping targets. It would then draw in the observer, submerge, and strike. The theory was sound, but in practice it lacked effectiveness. One of the first manned kites was battle-tested from a submarine operating north of Madagascar. The kite and its rider were launched into the air several times, but the risk proved too great. Each time the spotter kite reached its optimum altitude, it was itself spotted by antisubmarine planes and had to be pulled in quickly in order for the submarine to dive and escape. The giro kite was designed to be cut loose if the observer's telephone report gave the submarine cause to crash-dive. The observer would then jettison the windmill, open a backpack parachute, and take his chances floating in the open ocean.

The discovery of this particular observer system caused some consternation among the Allies before it became obvious that the use of such equipment greatly increased the vulnerability of the submarines. And its use was particularly ironic for Royal Air Corps Wing Commander Brie, who was considered England's greatest expert on rotary-wing flight. Long before the war broke out, he developed a toy windmill kite which worked on exactly the same principle as the German U-boat device. The war had prevented his toy from being put on the market.

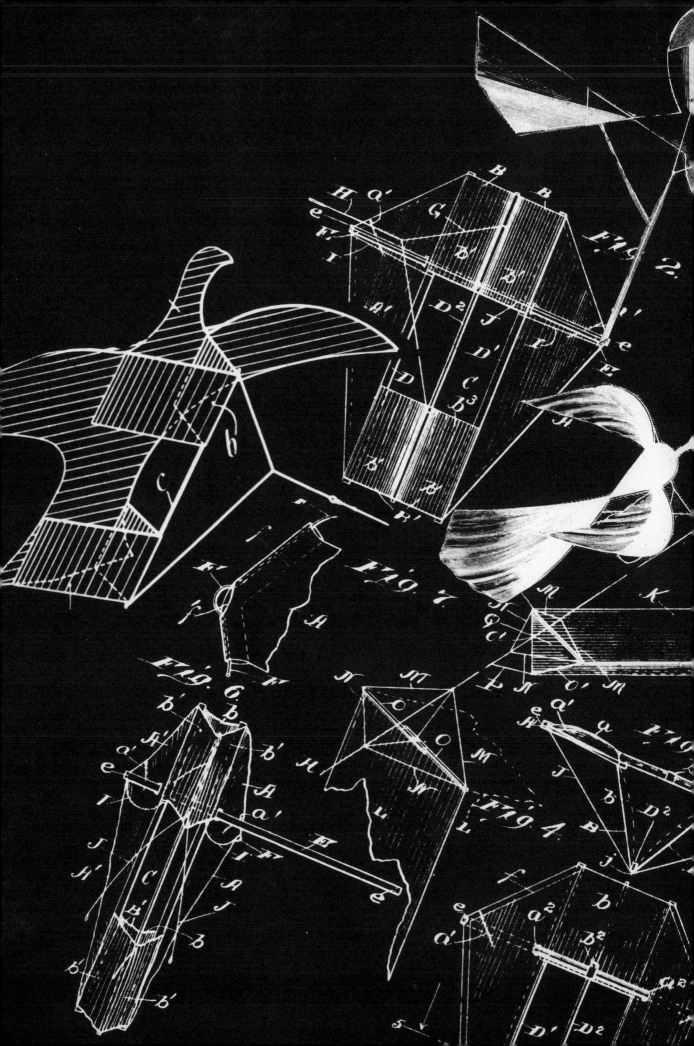

# Dr. Bell's Kites

◆ "The word kite unfortunately is suggestive to most minds of a toy," wrote Alexander Graham Bell, inventor of the telephone, in a 1907 article in the *National Geographic*. However, for more than ten years beginning in 1898 Dr. Bell focused his tremendous mind and energy in the direction of kites. His experiments played an important part in the establishment of several of the aerodynamic principles that made motored flight possible.

After the Wright brothers' successful airplane flight in 1903, Dr. Bell's work and that of his associates shifted slightly and was aimed at making flight safe and efficient. During the years of experimentation at Cape Breton, Nova Scotia, Bell produced the "tetra," which, with the Hargrave box kite and the Eddy bowed two-stick kite, became a lasting innovation in kite design. He then multiplied this innovation into some of the most efficient and majestic kites ever to fly. "These structures were really aerial vehicles," wrote Bell. "They were flown after the manner of kites, but their flying cords were stout manila ropes . . . anchored to the ground by several turns around stout cleats, like those employed in steamships and men-of-war."

Dr. Bell viewed his flight work as being divided into three stages—the kite stage, the motorboat stage, and the free flying-machine stage. And it was early in the kite stage that he began producing the "tetra." He was seeking a method to overcome the weight-to-lift relationship that proved a major handicap to most early flight pioneers. He reasoned that if the weight of a structure could be controlled and increased in relation to an equal expansion in flying surface, an effective flying machine could be constructed. The basic flying unit consisted of six rods of equal length connected into the form of a pyramid with four equal surfaces. This connection provided maximum strength with a minimum of material. By covering two adjoining faces with silk, or other light and durable material, Bell had a "winged cell" that could become an element of a much larger compound structure. It was then a matter of attaching similar cell to similar cell and constructing massive and still flyable structures. Test kites of 2, 4, 8, 16, and finally 256 cells were successful.

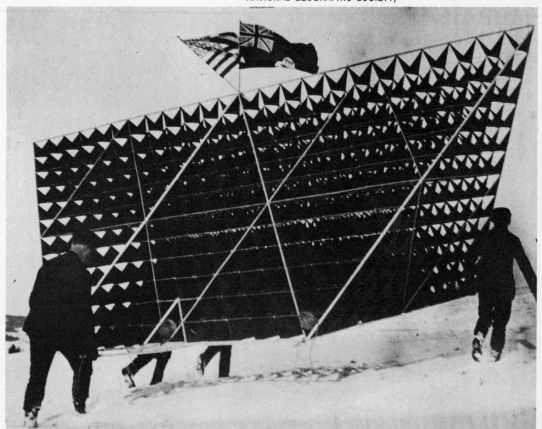

To test his theories further, Dr. Bell "put together into one structure all the available winged cells I had in the laboratory . . . thirteen hundred in number." The result was the Frost King, with successive layers of cells upon each other. The base layer consisted of twelve rows of thirteen cells each, attached to one another by their upper corners. The next layer had eleven rows of fourteen cells, the next, ten rows of fifteen cells, and each succeeding layer increased in width and decreased in breadth by a single unit. This tightly packed mass of winged cells weighing sixty-one pounds was finally sent up into the sky in a wind of less than ten miles per hour. It proved strong enough to support several long dangling ropes, a rope ladder, and a man. One of Dr. Bell's associates took hold of one of the dangling ropes and was raised to a height estimated at between thirty and forty feet.

The Frost King in flight (PHOTOGRAPH BY A. G. BELL, COURTESY AND
COPYRIGHT, THE BELL FAMILY AND NATIONAL GEOGRAPHIC SOCIETY)

The 3,393-cell Cygnet, ready for its first passenger flight, is towed by steamer into the center of Bras-d'Or Lake (PHOTOGRAPH BY JOHN McNEIL, COURTESY AND COPYRIGHT, NATIONAL GEOGRAPHIC SOCIETY)

Following the success of the Frost King, Bell and his Aerial Experimental Association made increasingly intricate and powerful structures in an attempt to move toward a self-sustained flying machine. In 1907, as the experiments were drawing to a close, the grandest of all of the Bell kite structures was completed. The Cygnet—measuring 13 meters across the top, 10 meters on the narrower bottom, standing 3 meters high, and containing 3,393 cellular flying units (nearly three times the size of the Frost King)—was ready for testing. Because of its immense size it was designed to be towed, aboard a small raft, by a steamboat in Baddeck Bay. Army Lieutenant Thomas Selfridge, one of motored flight's early heroes, had been working with Dr. Bell and the aerial association for some time and was to be the first passenger on the Cygnet. It was Bell's hope that a Cygnet-style wing would eventually

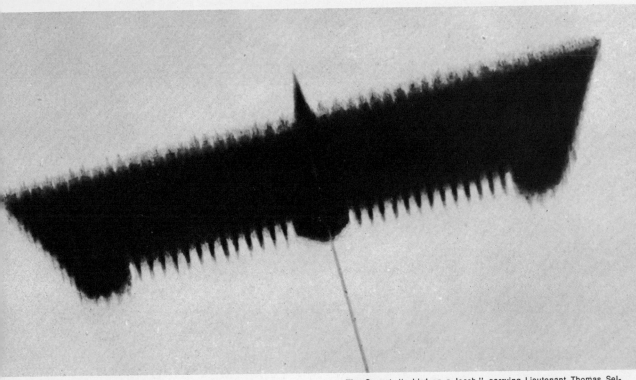

The Cygnet, "a bird on a leash," carrying Lieutenant Thomas Selfridge to an altitude of 168 feet (PHOTOGRAPH BY JOHN DAVIDSON, COURTESY AND COPYRIGHT, NATIONAL GEOGRAPHIC SOCIETY)

carry its own motor and pilot and would be able, after a kite-style launching, to drop the groundline and fly on its own power.

On December 6, 1907, with Lieutenant Selfridge tucked into an open space near the base of the structure, the Cygnet was towed down Baddeck Bay by the steamship. It swept to an altitude of 168 feet, held at that height for a few minutes, and then descended gracefully to a soft landing on the bay. A few moments after this successful and safe flight the Cygnet was severely damaged while being towed toward the Bell landing. Although Dr. Bell was not the first to accomplish motored flight, his contribution to the modern flight age is of great significance. Among the many inventions developed by his Aerial Experimental Association was the first wing-tip hinged aileron, an innovation that soon became standard on airplanes.

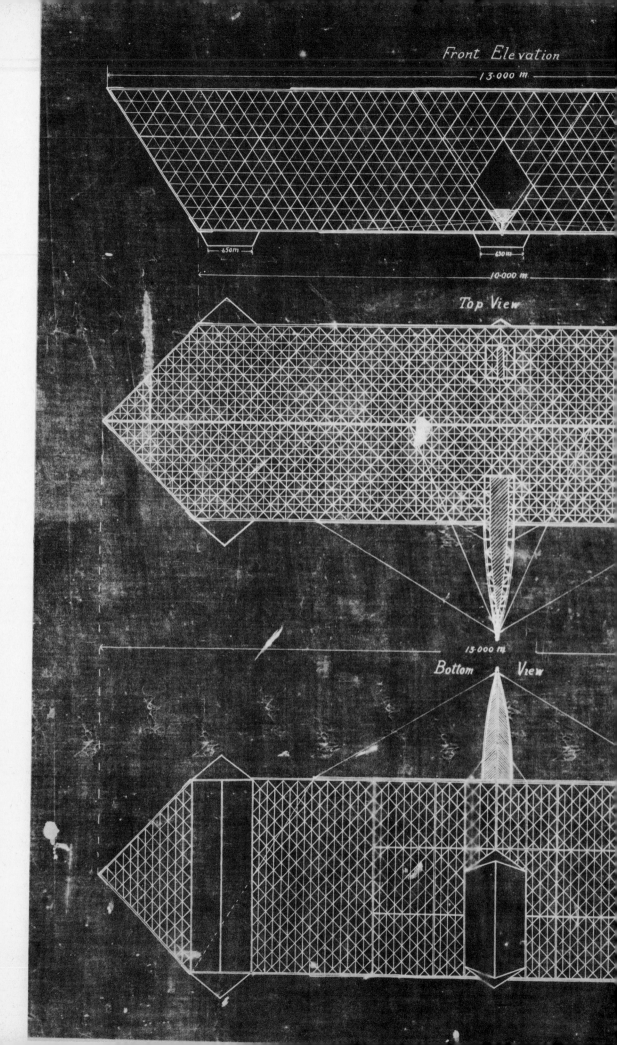

Front Elevation

13.000 m.

650m.  650 m.

10.000 m.

Top View

13.000 m.

Bottom View

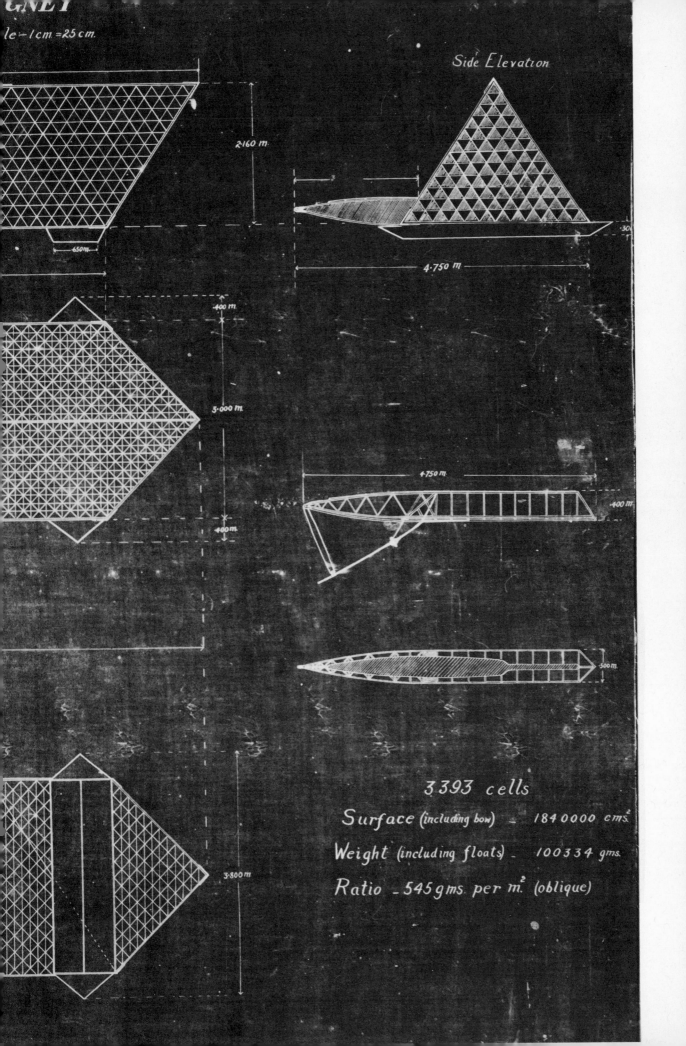

*GNET*

*le—1cm =25 cm.*

2·160 m.

650 m.

Side Elevation

4·750 m.

30

400 m.

3·000 m.

400 m.

4·750 m.

400 m.

500 m.

3·800 m.

*3393 cells*

*Surface* (including bow) — *184 0000 cms.²*

*Weight* (including floats) — *100334 gms.*

*Ratio —545 gms. per m.² (oblique)*

# Kites Without Wind

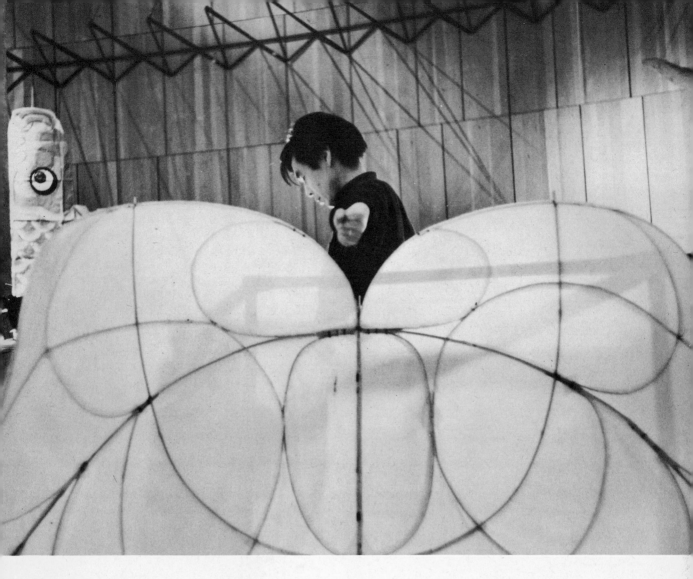

◆ When Fumio Yoshimura was a five-year-old child living in a Japanese seaside village, he flew a kite and "felt the sensation of having the wind in my hand." Thirty years later, living and working as an artist in the United States, he, through a series of unplanned events, began to be known as a kite sculptor.

He made his first kite-shaped object in 1963, more or less as a whim. He had visited an artificial flower show at the New York Coliseum and purchased some strips of Japanese bamboo. He later shaped them into an intricate frame by carefully bending the thin bamboo strips in bows and tying the loops against one another so that the combined stresses gave strength to the framework. He then covered the frame with rice paper and painted the shape with acrylics. It ended up looking like a kite, and during the next few months he continued experimenting with bamboo, creating

"shaped canvases" which, although they were not designed for flying, could only be called kite objects. During this period he was introduced as a kite sculptor to Marcel DuChamp who was visiting New York. DuChamp asked to see some of his objects, and within the next few days Fumio created four small "kites." DuChamp was impressed by the work and encouraged him to continue with the forms.

Before becoming involved in making kite objects, Fumio Yoshimura had been a painter. His work with bamboo structures led to increasingly involved shapes containing remarkable implied motion, and he gradually began to leave his painting and concentrate on sculpture. In 1964 the Museum of Contemporary Crafts put together an exhibition called "Amusements." Yoshimura, commissioned to create an object, produced a fourteen-foot-long moth shape. The "Amusements" exhibi-

tion, sponsored by the American Federation of Art, toured the United States for two years, and at the completion of the tour the Yoshimura "kite" was added to the Crafts Museum's permanent collection. Since 1964 Fumio Yoshimura's kite sculptures have become widely known and have grown in complexity while retaining all of the lightness and freedom of the simplest flying kite. In time his main focus as a sculptor has expanded to larger structural objects, but the quality of kites and flight has become an integral part of all of his work.

In the summer of 1965 Fumio began teaching a course at the Brookfield Art Center in Connecticut. The first summer the course was titled "Bamboo Kite Construction," although he had not actually flown a kite since his childhood in Japan. Toward the end the class grew anxious to test out the flying abilities of their fragile objects. The class, but not the instructor, was disappointed when rains forced them to call off the test flights. The following year the name of the course was changed, by the instructor, to "Bamboo Sculpture and Mobiles." It wasn't until 1967 that Yoshimura actually tried to fly

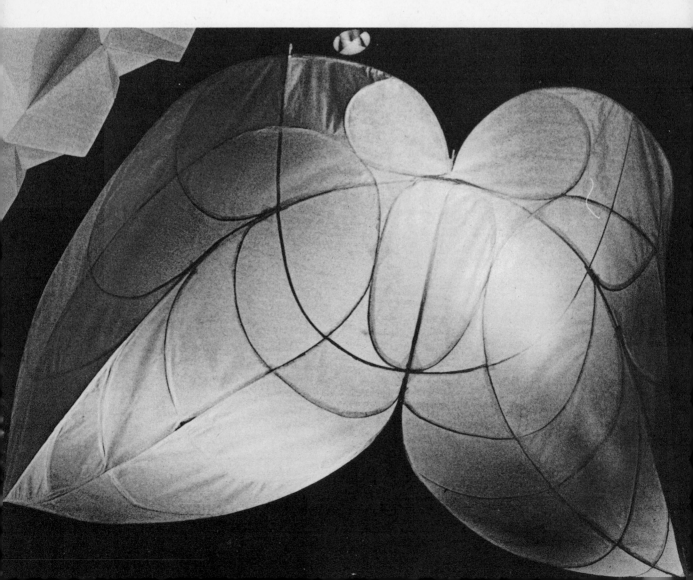

anything made by his own hands. Vacationing on Cape Cod with his wife, sculptress Kate Millet, he tentatively lofted his first flying kite into the air and again felt the sensation of having the wind in his hand. He spent the next five days constantly flying small kites.

The "1968 Paper Show" of the Museum of Contemporary Crafts, which toured the country, contained twenty-two elegant kites sculptured in the form of moths, manta rays, beetles, and birds by Fumio Yoshimura. They ranged in size from an eleven-inch bug to a sixteen-by-eighteen-foot floating wing, and although not built to fly at the end of a kite-line, the structures were such that each could more than hold its own in the sky.

As his work as a sculptor has broadened and he has become involved with new forms, the "kites" have become a "relaxation" and a source of ideas for other sculptures. The kite objects mirror his thought that this area of his work "is itself a sort of high-degree play" and that "nonsense art, either in rhetoric or through manipulations, requires serious approaches and time and real labor, but the satisfaction, the joy, is tremendous."

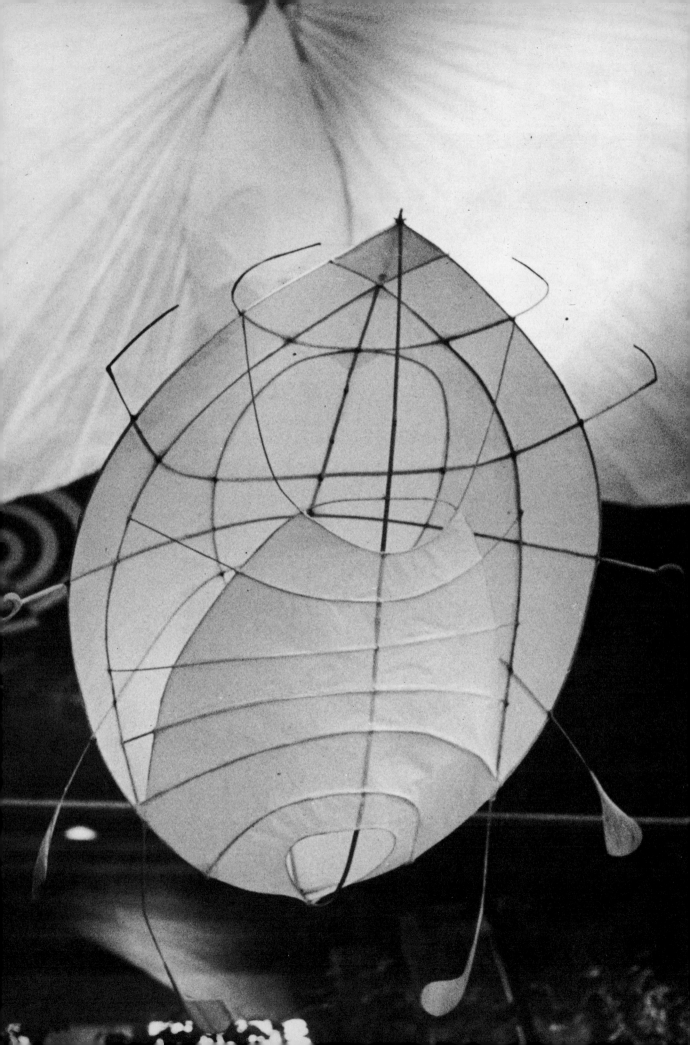

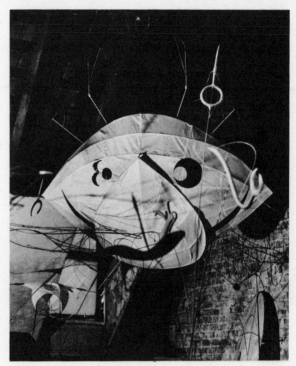

◆ Al Hansen's big, bright, striped kite canvases are representative of the pop art world's reaction to kites in the 1960s. Hansen, a co-founder with Allan Kaprow and Claes Oldenburg of that hybrid art form, the "happening," a painter, and an experimental art instructor at Rutgers University, surprised himself with his first flag kite canvas in 1965. He had been working for some time on a series of small fragment paintings called "Views of Old Glory as Seen Through a Speakeasy Door." He was living in a slightly renovated barn in Provincetown on Cape Cod and bought an armload of fifteen-cent, two-stick kites at the grocery for use as wall decorations. Hanging them up, he became fascinated with two standard American flag-decorated kites. He stretched large canvases into the shape of the kites, began painting, and within two weeks had half a dozen, six- to eight-foot paintings of flags, frankfurters, comic-strip heroes, and Hershey bar wrappers.

Since the initial kite painting, his work has been added to a number of private collections and a twelve-foot kite-shaped canvas of a giant rocket ship burbling through deep space hangs in Provincetown's Chrysler Museum. Plans and work on other kite-canvas subjects continue—a seventeen-foot-high Union Jack with the Beatles that splits down the center for use as a very large door painting; a Chinese dragon-style kite with each round surface telling a chapter of Jayne Mansfield's life, beginning with her first film role and ending with her tragic auto accident; giant Brigitte Bardot and Joey Heatherton portrait kites; and stars and flags and flags with hot dogs. Although he flies real kites without the least trace of self-consciousness, he has been a source of confusion to truck drivers and construction workers in Manhattan's Lower East Side. It is not an uncommon sight for Al Hansen to be spotted walking down the street from his studio loft toward an art gallery balancing an eight- to twelve-foot kite-shaped painting of the stars and stripes.

"Hey, buddy, you gonna fly that?"

"Of course, what else is a kite for?"

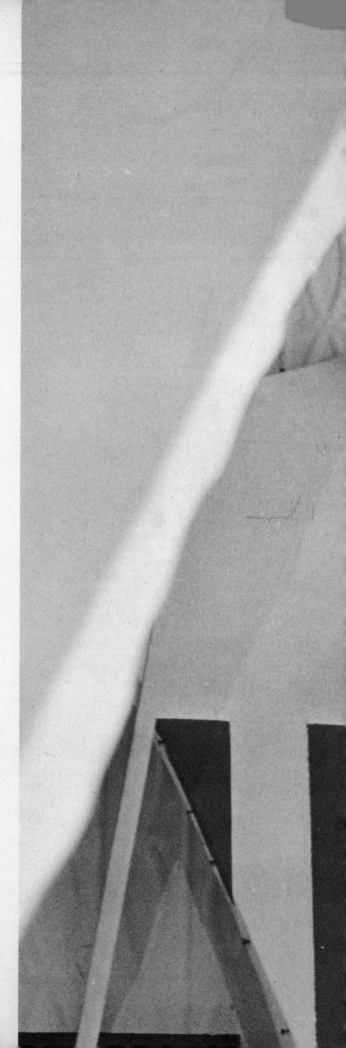

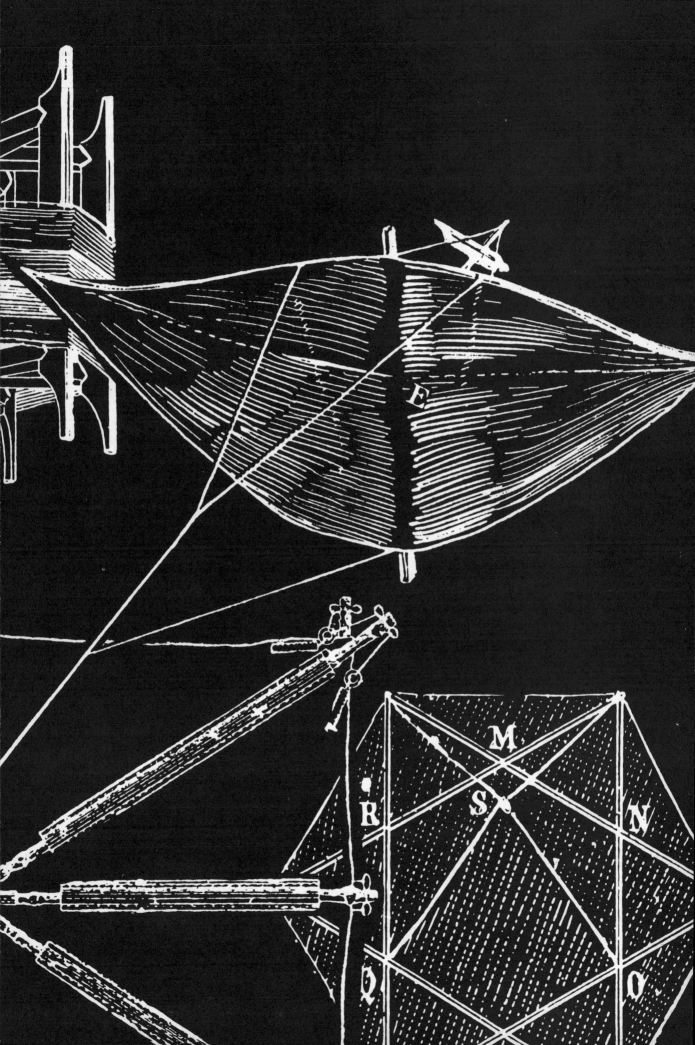

# Two Kiteflyers from Columbus

David Thayer's (1898) proposed oceangoing k
and raft

Benn Blinn

◆ Walter Scott and Benn Blinn, after driving up and down the perimeter roads of Nantucket Island, off Massachusetts' Cape Cod coast, finally stopped at a quiet stretch of beach near the village of Siasconset. Parking Scott's station wagon at the end of a sandy road that opened onto the beach, they began unloading equipment. Light fog was coming in off the Atlantic in puffs as Blinn swiftly carried a light blue hand-crafted wood gear frame and placed it on top of a well-weathered beach trash basket. Walter Scott, only a step behind, fitted a hand drill into the frame, returned to the car, brought out a large steel spool of five thousand feet of monofilament fishing line, and locked it into place on the frame. A ten-year-old boy pedaled down the road on his bicycle, stared for a moment at the two bearded men, and asked if they had seen a dachshund. Scott smiled, "No, not today." The boy propped his bicycle against an embankment and sat down in the sand to watch what was happening.

A five-foot-long black kite was unfurled, and Benn Blinn began the job of inserting sticks into its box-frame center, arranged the cross struts to support the side wings, and adjusted the kite's bridle with half blood knots. Working with glove-covered hands, he tied the spool line to the bridle and walked slowly toward the surf with the polyethylene kite fluttering in his hands. He held the kite into the gusty offshore wind blowing toward the northeast and began working it up into the air. It flew smoothly, picking up speed and pulling line from the spinning spool at its own pace. At four hundred feet the kite began to yaw inland, fought for a brief moment, then

The Scott-Blinn transocean sea anchor

coasted up into the fog out over the water, and rose easily for several hundred more feet, occasionally becoming visible through the fog-shrouded twilight. The only sound was that of the surf washing the beach and the wind sweeping seaward over the dunes. Blinn tightened his gloved grip on the line. "We should be up about a thousand feet now, Scotty. You got the message ready?"

Walter Scott finished writing his note: "This kite was launched on June 23 at 6:45 p.m. EST from Nantucket Island, U.S.A. en route to England. If found please notify Benn Blinn and Walter Scott, Columbus, Ohio, and we will send you the other half of the enclosed portion of a dollar bill." The message and torn bill were placed into a glazed, plastic half-gallon detergent bottle which Blinn tied to the kite-line. The kite pulled the bottle up forty feet, and Blinn again held the line fast. The line was cut from the spool and tied to a yellow plastic bucket. Blinn took a firm grip on the bucket, and the men walked across the beach to the water's edge. The boy got up from his place in the sand and followed slightly behind them. The bucket with the kite-line straining at the handle was placed into the water and freed. Two breaking waves kept it in near the sand until, suddenly, the kite took charge and began towing the partially filled bucket out into the sea. The boy looked up at Walter Scott and asked what they were doing.

"We're flying kites to England. We're going to be the first men to ever do it."

The boy nodded solemnly, "Gee, you're going to be famous."

"No, no" said Walter, "we're just two old men who love kites."

Benn Blinn, who could easily be mistaken for Pan, and Walter Scott, who has often been mistaken for Ernest Hemingway and Santa Claus, began flying kites together in the late 1950s. Blinn was the first to become deeply involved in the subject after receiving a standard fifteen-cent kite from his wife, Lee, on her birthday in 1957. Unable to keep it in the air, he went into his workshop, made his own, and it flew. He was a kiteflyer, and in 1959 he introduced Walter Scott to the sport. That same year they shared the dream of sending anchor-towing kites similar to the J. Woodbridge Davis buoy-towing kite system (Chapter II) across an ocean.

The Blinns live on a forty-acre "shrub and Halloween pumpkin" farm that sits as an island in the heart of Columbus' Arlington suburb. Since the kiteflying started, the property has served as the prime testing location for the Blinn and Scott kites and has become a familiar spot for several Federal Aviation Agency investigators who blame most of the area's unidentified flying object reports on the big kites sent up from the site.

The Nantucket adventure was the second attempt to send kites scudding across the ocean. A year earlier the two men journeyed from Columbus to Nova Scotia and launched half a dozen kites into the waves only to watch five break up in the heavy winds. But one was reported found two hundred miles up the coast and the men vowed to repeat their

attempt the following summer. En route to Nova Scotia they had visited New York's Central Park where they plugged in their electric rewind units, through a three-hundred-foot-long extension cord, to a comfort station that sits atop a knoll at the edge of the Sheep Meadow. The extension cord and the electric rewinding machine have freed them from the exhausting chore of hand-reeling in up to three miles of kite-line.

From Central Park they were off up the East Coast, pausing to find a socket and fly in the Boston Common and, a day later to plug into a swimming pool patio outlet in Bar Harbor, Maine. In Bar Harbor they learned that a UFO had been sighted at roughly the same time that their kite was in the air. An interview by a part-time Associated Press reporter resulted in newspaper stories throughout the country about two men who were being "towed to Europe on their kites," and Walter Scott's wife, Jane, spent two days answering telephone calls and assuring questioners that Scotty was not floating out over the ocean hanging from a kite.

The interview and subsequent newspaper coverage, while a surprise to the men, was not their first brush with the press. Their first publicity came in 1960 during an unsuccessful attempt to fly a kite, while retaining control of the line, over an international border. They had journeyed to Puffin Bay near Sandusky, Ohio, with the intention of putting one up over the narrow point of Lake Erie to Canada. Instead, northerly winds held their kites over Ohio and caused several UFO reports. When a small story appeared two days later in the Sandusky paper, the men agreed that kites made a good addition to the newspaper and began a never-ending game aptly called "one above the fold." To win at "one above the fold," a headline concerning a kite exploit must be discovered on the top half of a newspaper front page. Page two or three is fair, but anything farther back in the body of the paper is not considered significant.

Their most dramatic success with the game came from their own kites three years after the Sandusky flight without their leaving the Blinn farm. An afternoon was spent getting three five-foot kites up on the same line at four-thousand-foot intervals. Toward dusk the tremendous pull of the three kites snapped the line, and the flyers called it a day. Charles Redman of Newark, Ohio, forty miles east of Columbus, was sitting down at the dinner table when he glanced out of a window and spotted what appeared to be a parachute caught in the top of an apple tree. Investigating, he discovered a nylon line leading up to the shape, pulled to no avail, picked up an ax, and chopped the tree down. Having never before chopped down a tree to find a kite with another line leading straight up into a darkening sky, he telephoned the Newark sheriff who soon appeared on the scene with ten

deputies. Using a garden hose reel to assist in the winding, they began pulling and in midevening drew in a second kite, only to find still more line extending skyward. The third and final object was on the ground shortly after midnight. Inspecting it, the sheriff discovered a sticker on the kite's wing with the wording: "Reward. Call Benn Blinn, Columbus. Don't Tangle String!" "One above the fold" in Newark. Page three in Columbus.

The Nantucket kites were similar to the winged box kites that were the center of the Newark incident, although the materials as well as the Nantucket launch site were influenced by a U.S. Weather Bureau prediction. The bureau, contacted shortly after the kite-flyers returned from their Nova Scotia trip, suggested that, assuming the kites could be built of sufficient strength to hold together for at least forty-three days and that the line could hold onto a light sea anchor to keep the line taut, the kites could theoretically make it across the ocean. The Weather Bureau suggested that Nantucket or nearby Martha's Vineyard serve as a beginning point and confirmed that the combination of winds and ocean currents could ultimately carry the bucket-towing kites smack into the middle of England's Southampton harbor.

The oceangoing kite launched in the evening fog and the sixteen that followed it over the horizon during the next three days ranged in height from five to ten feet and were witnessed by puzzled onlookers who quickly turned into boosters. The observers kept up a constant flow of questions which have, over the years, become familiar to the men. Blinn fielded the technical questions and waved the queries concerning the mood of the thing to Walter Scott. "No, no" said Walter Scott when asked if they were doing it for advertising, "we're just two men who love to fly kites."

At the midpoint of the launching, with eight kites off in the direction of England, Benn Blinn decided that it was time to put up a celebration kite for the Nantucket townspeople. Walter Scott decided that it was time to take a predinner nap. Returning to their island headquarters, the Ships Inn, Blinn enlisted the willing aid of Tim Clark and half a dozen vacationers and made his way up to the widow's walk. With the extension cord trailing down a narrow stairway to a hall plug, he launched an eight-foot orange kite. Within minutes he was walking down the cobblestone main street asking strollers and loungers what they thought "it" was.

"It's a flying orange donut, Baby," "Must be a weather balloon; they go up every day at this time."

Benn Blinn puts up a "Halloween" kite over the town of Nantucket

Observers, led by Blinn (right), react

He walked the length of the street, stopping finally at the harbor's edge, and studied the orange dot barely visible through the dusk. He was pleased with an explanation offered by an attractive girl who pedaled slowly by on a bicycle. "It looks like an eerydescent UDO to me!"

At noon on June 26 the last kite took its place in the line and moved steadily out of view. Twenty-four hours later, America's greatest kite team, pausing in their drive back to Columbus to await word on their adventure, cruised the quiet streets of Newport, Rhode Island, looking for electricity. They spotted a plug on a telephone pole adjacent to the Jamestown Ferry but it was dead, tried the town waterworks adjacent to an open lot and were turned down by a puzzled supervisor, and finally received a go-ahead from the bartender of the Newport Yacht Club to make use of a dockside outlet. With the wind registering less than a knot on the club's wind meter, Benn Blinn gently worked a nine-foot black kite into the air. A dozen sailors, working on their boats while waiting for the nearly absent breeze to pick up, stopped to watch the two bearded men. A delivery man, on his way out of the clubhouse, paused for a moment and asked, "You guys rainmakers?"

"No, no," said Walter Scott, "we're just two men who love to fly kites, and we want to do it in every state in the country."

Four months after the successful and exciting launch the men agreed that the attempt would have to be repeated. The only kite reported found was pulled in by a tuna fisherman a week after the send-off, at a point 35 miles and 150° off Nantucket. During the waiting period they had answered the fan mail from England that resulted from a page-three report of the flight in the London *Mirror*. The story referred to them as millionaires, and their mail was filled with offers of homes for sale, sporting opportunities to finance family reunions, and invitations to come and stay for awhile.

Kites keep flying over the Blinn "farm," and Walter Scott continues to spend the winter months putting his kites up over the inland waterway near his seasonal home in Delray Beach, Florida. The plans for new adventures continue to take shape. The Atlantic crossing —it'll succeed, and there has been talk of boarding the cruise ship that now makes a once-a-year trip to Antarctica. It wouldn't be too surprising if a "one above the fold" someday soon tells of a slightly frozen kite, tied to a yellow bucket, being spotted making a right turn out of the Humboldt Current heading with determination toward the Panama Canal's southern entrance.

# Instructions for Building and Flying Twelve Kites

◆ Kites fly because they are, or contain, inclined planes or flat surfaces, held up by the power of the wind. And every flyable kite is an airfoil whose efficiency is a result of the lift and drag forces created by the kite's shape and flying angle.

The most basic kite is the familiar two-stick diamond shape. Angled upward in the air at the nose and held in that position by the bridle, it is struck by the wind. Part of the wind moves over the top of the inclined plane, and part moves underneath it. The flow over the top moves faster than the air directly behind the kite's leading edge and creates a vacuum. This causes lift. The air, flowing underneath the kite, is forced downward along the depressed plane and, attempting to fill the vacuum above the kite, completes the lifting effect. In this effort, however, it also creates a drag force by pushing against the angled plane. The ultimate, getting a kite to fly, is achieved by getting it properly angled in the air so that the lift exceeds the drag.

Nearly any object with flat surfaces will fly if its weight is not too great for its potential lift; for example, a common shoe box. Tape a cover on it, fasten an angled bridle to the box, and attach a lead line to the bridle. It will oscillate and roll around, but if there is sufficient wind, it will fly. If the box is discarded and an attempt is made to try to fly only the cover, it will fly a bit better. The flanges of the cover will, however, still set up a considerable drag. If the flanges are trimmed off, leaving a flat cardboard shape, and a tail is added, it will fly quite well. It now has the same lift as the original shoe box and lid but has less drag and less weight.

If this cardboard rectangle were trimmed into a diamond shape, creased down the middle to give it dihedral, or upward-inclined, wings, it would fly still better. If it were left in its flat rectangular shape and a V-vent cut just back of the middle, it would stabilize more effectively. Otherwise, because it has no laterals, or fins, to keep it directed straight into the wind, it requires a considerable amount of tail, or balance, to keep it flying in a stable position.

The Eddy kite (folio kite 2) is a diamond-shape kite with refinements brought about by William Eddy to eliminate the need for a tail. He accomplished this by broadening the kite so that the width was equal, or nearly equal, to its length and by bowing the cross-stick to gain lateral stability. The bowing of an Eddy kite forms a semilateral effect at the wings tips, resulting in a kite of considerable airworthiness.

A slightly different advantage from that gained by the Eddy kite is a significant element of the Scott Sled (folio kite 10) and is a result of venting. If a coin is dropped into water, it will oscillate back and forth all the way to the bottom. A ball bearing dropped in the same water will fall smoothly and, barring current, in a straight line. This is a result of an even distribution of force on the ball bearing's surface. Unequal forces are built up on the coin's flat surface during its descent. The coin will move about to escape these forces since it is subject to basic gravitational effects. The coin, developing less pressure on its top surface than on its bottom surface, experiences turbulence which causes the oscillation. This example can be applied to a kite. The smoother the air flow around its surfaces, the better and more stably it will fly. This is why the Scott Sled is vented. Since it canopies downward and its side flaps become laterals, the air is vented through the V-hole cut slightly beyond the midpoint of the canopy, and the air flow is smooth. No turbulence of any significance is developed over its top plane.

Lawrence Hargrave's box kite takes advantage of both stability and lateral control. It was the search for optimum flying efficiency that resulted in his development of this now-familiar kite (folio kite 8). The advantage of the box kite is that its "sidewalls," necessary to achieve the box shape, form perfect laterals in addition to creating four plane surfaces and an efficient venting in the kite's midsection. Turbulence would develop if the kite were made into a single surface containing the same area of the combined planes. Instead, a maximum lift is gained without turbulence. The only drag force on a box kite, other than that normally generated by the flow of air on its undersides, is from the framing. The Scott Sled, without lateral spars, has virtually no drag other than that of the wind force meeting its underside.

Flying line is the one drag force which is constant with all kites. Line drag force increases according to the length of the line and the amount of the wind. Smooth lines will minimize the drag effect. The old grocery. twine, often used, is one of the worst lines in this respect because of its fuzz which creates a large amount of additional drag.

The Para-Foil (folio kite 12) is a magnificent example of proper lift-to-drag ratio. Most kiteflyers prefer kites without tails. Some, however, fascinated by the exotic-shaped kites that require tails, know that a kite tail is used not to add stabilizing weight but to add balance.

## Lines

The discovery of nylon and other synthetic materials, now used for kite lines, was a boon to kiteflyers all over the world. It is remarkable that pioneers like Eddy and Hargrave efficiently and successfully flew kites without them. Stories are told of how binder twine used to be hoarded by boys in order to loft their kite creations. A current-day kiteflyer would shudder, even give up kiting, if he had to go back to the old lines. Grocery twine broke under the slightest pressure and had weight out of proportion to its strength. Nylon lines are now the most popular and are scaled by their diameter and the break strength they possess. A 450-pound test line measures one-eighth of an inch in diameter and, under proper conditions, can withstand any pull up to 450 pounds. A 700-pound test line, seldom used except on giant Para-Foils, is 3/16 of an inch in diameter. Great strength is gained in a mere sixteenth-of-an-inch nylon line. An equivalent break strength in manila line would cause it to be too heavy to be successfully used for flying kites.

There are many excellent kite lines available in lighter weights. Braided rather than twisted fibers are preferred. The average kite needs no more than 20- or 30-pound line. Light models, such as the Scott Sled, can be flown on monofilament lines ranging in strength from 4- to 18-pound test. A monofilament line is so named because it is a single strand of nylon or other synthetic material.

There are many fine-braided fishlines that make good kite lines, but it is difficult to find them of sufficient length. Larger spools of such line can usually be found in the major mail-order catalogs. If several spools or lengths of line are knotted together, the blood knot should be used. The blood knot is tied by looping the end of one line around the line to which it is being joined, then looping it back around itself, and finally tucking it back through the opening where it rounds the other line. This creates a sliding noose and lessens the strain on the line if the lines slip in different directions. The ends of nylon line should be burned to prevent fraying.

## Launching a Kite

Since the weight and drag of the flying line are important elements of stability, a kite will fly best when it has line weight upon it. It is best to get the kite up and out as quickly as possible. A small-or medium-sized kite should launch from the hand. It should "drift" far enough away to get it up safely. It should "drift" with some line tension, not so little that it loses wind power and falls, and not so much that it climbs rapidly and loops over into a power dive. Almost any kite will oscillate on a short line since it overpowers the balancing effect. Letting out additional line adds balance and pulls the bridle line down into proper position.

When launching a large kite, it is best to have someone carry it out one hundred or more feet and then free it. If flying alone, it's necessary to do an excellent job of line handling. Few kites will remain upright in the wind if not held, so the lone flyer must launch by holding the kite in his hand, freeing it, and letting out line as fast as the kite can take the line without losing altitude. The line should be run through the hand and "braked" down accordingly. And when flying powerful kites, gloves, should be worn.

When the kite has reached a good altitude, the running line should be "snubbed" to a halt slowly. Stopping it abruptly tends to put stress on the kite and the line and makes the kite fly erratically. If the pull on the line feels reasonably gentle and the kite flies evenly and well for a few minutes, more line can be fed out and the kite can be flown as high as desired.

## Landing

Landing a kite, especially a big kite, can be difficult. Even winding in a small diamond kite on a hand held winder can be a tiresome experience.

Winding in a kite increases the wind power upon its surface. The increased wind power can cause the kite to "power loop" and crash to the ground. To avoid this, the kite can be "walked down." This is done by tying the line to a tree or post and walking toward the kite, letting the line slide under gloved hands. This method of bringing a kite down does not substantially increase the wind power, for the kite is being lowered instead of being dragged directly through the air. It's obvious that a kite cannot be walked all the way down if one is in a field five hundred feet long and has a kite flying at the end of fifteen hundred feet of line. In this case the flyer should walk as far as he can, then hold the line and walk slowly back to the starting point. By walking backward he can keep an eye on the kite and slacken the line if the kite appears to be losing stability. When back at the starting point, he can tie off the line again and repeat the walk until the kite is over the field for the final walk all the way down. If a flyer has a reel that will take in line smoothly and without much effort, it shouldn't be necessary for him to walk a kite down. But even slow and steady reeling increases the wind power and can cause the kite to lose stability.

## Building Kites

The kites described and illustrated on the following pages are, with the exception of the Miniature Navy Barrage Kite, quite easy to build and fly. They represent the basic kite shapes. By simply changing the dimensions while staying with the stated proportions, one can build them to various sizes. These kites can also serve as the basis for a kite-builder's own variations on shapes as can be seen by glancing again at the kites built and flown by Walter Scott, Benn Blinn, and Tomi Ungerer. The only equipment needed consists of a ruler or tape measure, strong, light-weight glue, nails, string, a pair of scissors or cutting blade, the suggested sticks, and covering material. There are no rules for kite-building. The only requirement is a desire to build something that flies. And every kite in the folio will fly.

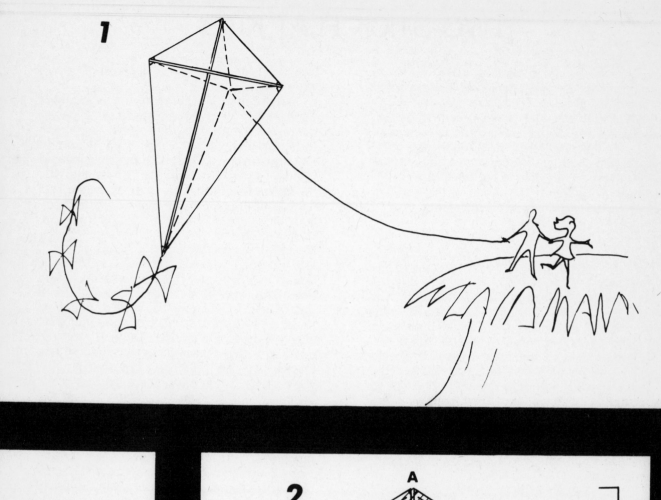

**1**

**3**

**2**

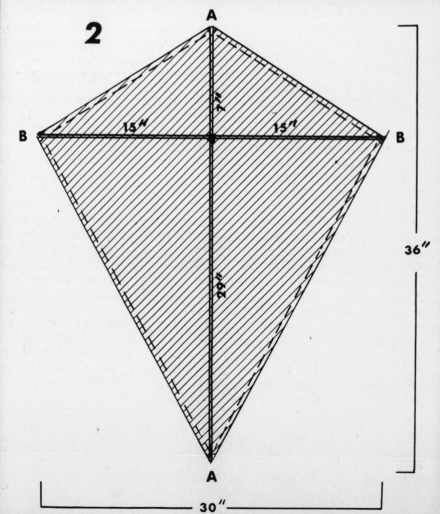

A

7"

B 15" 15" B

29"

36"

A

30"

# TWO-STICK FLAT KITE

1 (A) stick, ⅜″ x ½″ x 36″
1 (B) stick, ⅜″ x ½″ x 30″

Notch the ends of both the A and the B sticks. Cross the sticks and tie them together at a point 7 inches from the top of the A stick and at the midpoint of the B stick. Glue can be applied over the tied string to assure against slippage. Starting from the top of the A stick, tie and run a string from point to point around the kite. Loop and tie this framing string through each notched stick-end before running it on to the next stick. Tape or tie the notched ends (Diagram 3) once the string is in place.

Place the completed frame upon a paper or polyethylene sheet selected as the covering. The covering must be cut large enough to allow a ½-inch or ¾-inch flap to be turned over the framing string. The paper should be trimmed so that it does not cover the ends of the sticks. Spread glue or paste on the flaps, fold them over the string, and let the glue or paste dry.

This kite flies easily but almost always needs a tail for stability. The length and weight of the tail is dictated by the wind strength. Make the tail by attaching scraps of paper or cloth to a strong string. Attach the tail to the bottom of the kite.

Bridle the kite by tying a string between the ends of the B (cross) stick that, when pulled, reaches a point 4 to 6 inches in front of the crossed stick point. Run a second string between the ends of the A stick, long enough to tie to the B string at the point 6 inches in front of the crossed stick. Attach the flying string to this point. The bridle and the tail may have to be adjusted up or down depending upon the prevailing winds.

# TAILLESS MALAY (EDDY) KITE

Sticks: 2 (A) sticks, ⅜″ x ½″ x 42″

This is a version of the kite patented by photographer William Eddy in 1897. It is easy to build and flies extremely well.

Tie the sticks together at the midpoint of the cross stick and 9 inches down from the top of the vertical stick. Then tie string around the ends of the sticks in the same manner described for the flat two-stick kite.

Bend the cross stick 4 inches and tie securely. The kite is then ready to be covered with strong paper or cloth.

The bridle for this particular kite is 63 inches long. A rule of thumb to keep in mind when building Malay kites of various sizes is that the bridle string should be one and one-half times the length of the vertical stick. The bridle attaches to the point at which the sticks cross, and to the bottom of the vertical stick. The flying line should be tied approximately 80 percent of the distance up from the lower end of the bridle line. It can then be adjusted up or down, depending upon the strength of the wind.

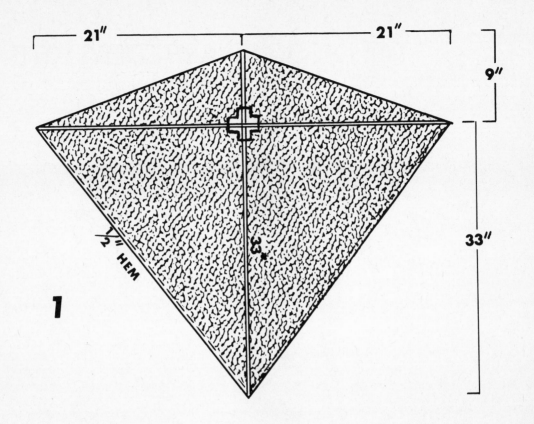

21″      21″

9″

33″

2″ HEM

33″

**1**

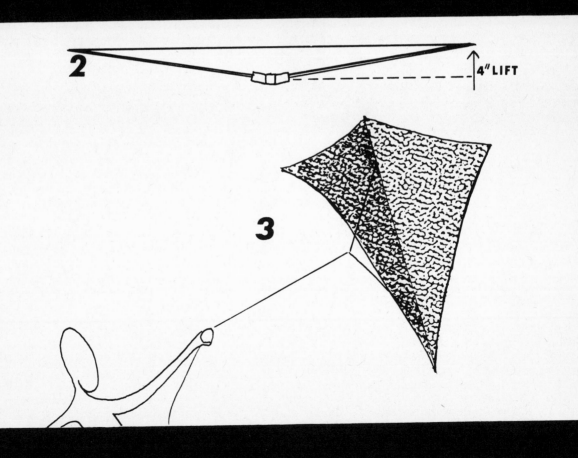

**2**

4″ LIFT

**3**

# RECTANGULAR JAPANESE KITE

1 (A) stick (thin bamboo or pine), 14″
1 (B) stick (bamboo or pine), 17½″
2 (C) sticks (bamboo or thin pine), 20¾″

The covering of this excellent flying kite should be of stiff wrapping paper or bark paper. Build the frame by crossing the C sticks at a point 11 inches from their top ends (Diagram 1). The B stick is then attached to the crossed C sticks at a point 8 inches from its top (the B stick) and 9½ inches from its lower end. Tie the three sticks together with string.

Lay the covering, measuring 14 inches by 17½ inches, flat. Place the A stick across the top of the covering and center its position, leaving ½ inch of covering exposed above the A stick. Spread glue over the flap and the stick, fold the flap down over the stick, and let it dry. The A stick should be extending ¾ inch from each outer edge of the covering material.

Lay the frame (crossed C sticks and B stick) on the back of the kite covering. The top of the B stick should reach to the middle of the lower edge of the A stick. The top ends of the C sticks should cross the A stick at the outside edges of the covering. Fix the frame to the covering by gluing the outside points of the frame to the covering and also gluing the cross-stick center point to the kite covering. Friction tape should then be placed over the points indicated in the diagram.

To fly this kite, bow the A stick (Diagram 2) 2 to 3 inches by stringing it between the points where the A stick and C sticks cross. Make a bridle by attaching strings to these same two points and bringing a line out from the kite's low-center crossed-stick point. The kite will fly well without a tail, but if it appears to be having difficulty remaining stable, a tail can be attached to the bottom end of the B stick.

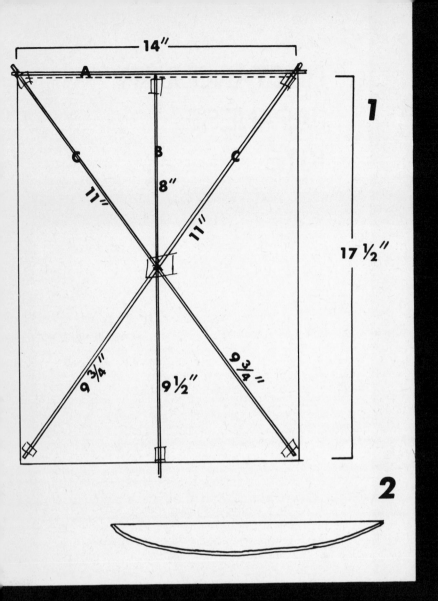

14"

A

B

8"

C — 11"

11" — C

17 1/2"

9 3/4"

9 1/2"

9 3/4"

**1**

**2**

**3**

音

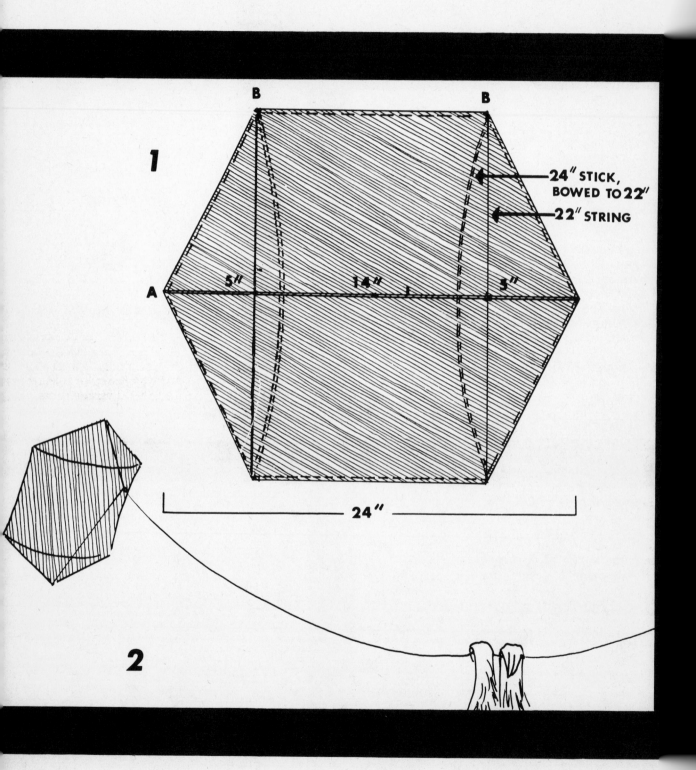

**1**

B                   B

24″ STICK,
BOWED TO 22″

22″ STRING

A      5″           14″           5″

24″

**2**

# 24-INCH DOUBLE-BOW KITE

1 (A) stick, ⅜″ x ½″ x 24″
2 (B) sticks, flexible and light, 24″

Mark the midpoint of the flexible B sticks. Bow them until a bowstring, running from end to end, measures 22 inches. Place the bowed B sticks (Diagram 1) bent toward each other with 14 inches between the bow strings. Lay the A stick across the bows, intersecting the bows, and extending 5 inches beyond each bowstring. Tie the bowstrings to the A stick at the points where they cross. Next, tie a string frame around the perimeter of the kite. Lay the completed frame upon the covering material (lightweight cloth is best for this kite), trim the material allowing for a ½-inch hem, fold the flap over the string frame, and fasten.

The bowed B sticks will be lying flat upon the covering. Force them up until they are facing forward into the covering. This gives the kite its double-bowed effect (Diagram 2). Make a bridle by running a string between the ends of the A stick, long enough to reach a point in the air 5 inches in front of the kite and 10 inches from the top of the A stick. Tie the flying line to this point. This kite does not need a tail.

# STUB
# NOSE
# KITE

2 (A) sticks, ⅜″ x ½″ x 30″
1 (B) stick, flexible, ⅛″ x ¼″ x 30″

Notch all sticks and mark the A sticks 8¾ inches from one end. Lay the A sticks one on top of the other, lined up with the marks, and tie them together at the marks with thread or string. Cross the sticks from the tied point until the lower ends of the sticks are 15½ inches apart. Tie and glue the crossed point firmly into position.

String the B stick into a bow with its bowstring measuring 21¾ inches between the ends of the stick. Place the A sticks over the bow with the string meeting the A sticks and the cross point and with the bowed stick pointing toward the lower ends of the sticks. Tie the midpoint of the bowstring to the cross point of the A sticks. Then, as described with the earlier kites, tie a string, starting from the top of either of the A sticks, around the perimeter of the kite. Place the completed kite frame on a cloth or paper covering, allowing for a ½-inch flap, fold the flap over the string, and glue it into position.

When the glue is completely dry, push the bowed stick into the covering until it is facing forward from the kite frame.

Attach the bridle line as shown in Diagram 2, with the flying string fixed at a point slightly beneath the point where the A sticks cross.

**1**

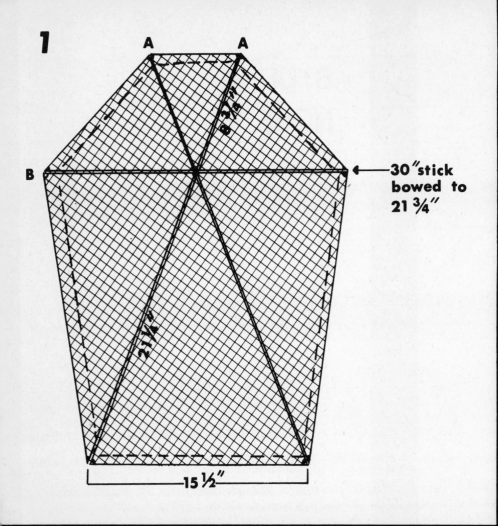

A    A

B

@ 3¾"

21½"

30" stick
bowed to
21 ¾"

15 ½"

**2**

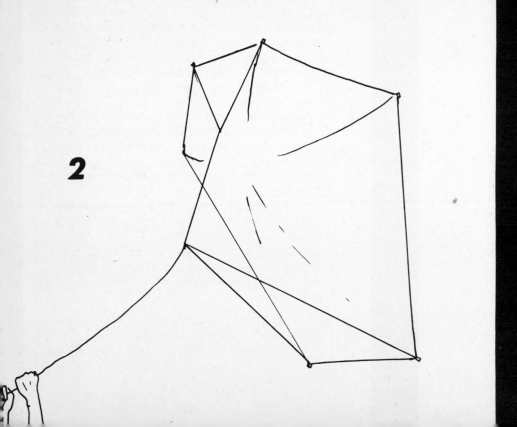

# BERMUDA HEAD-STICK KITE

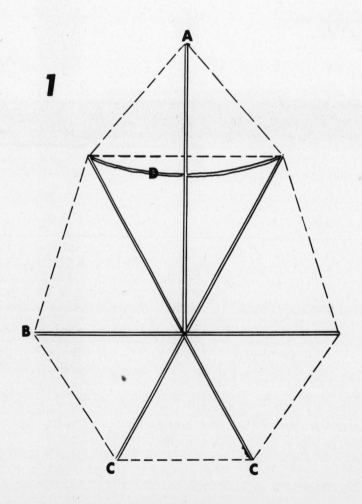

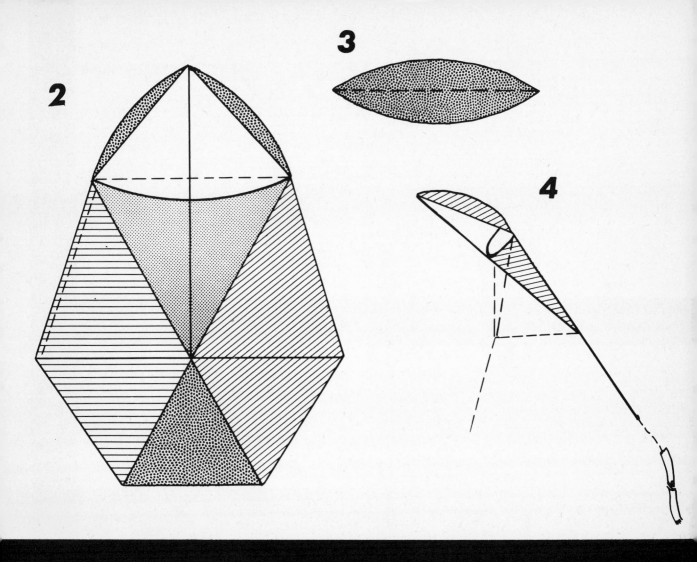

1 (A) stick, ⅜″ x ¼″ x 20″
1 (B) stick, ⅜″ x ¼″ x 22″
2 (C) sticks, ⅜″ x ¼″ x 24″
1 (D) stick, ¼″ bamboo 18″

Notch all sticks. Cut holes into one end of each of the C sticks on the ⅜-inch surface. These holes are used to attach the cane bow.

Place the sticks into position as shown in Diagram 1, with the A stick on top. Drive a nail through all four sticks at the bottom of the A stick. Place a piece of bowed bamboo into the holes at the tops of the C sticks, forcing the A stick up. Tie the A stick to the bamboo bow. Then tie string tightly from the top of one of the C sticks to the top of the bow stick and down to the top of the remaining C stick (Diagram 1). This will hold the head-stick (A) in position.

Run a second string around the entire kite, through the notched ends of the sticks, ex-cluding the top of the head-stick.

Paper the shaded portions of the kite (Diagram 2) with different colored tissues or cellophane. Measure the material by laying it on the frame, marking the sections with a light pencil or crayon. Trim the sections out with scissors, leaving a flap on the outer edges that can be tucked under the perimeter string. Spread glue along the sticks and lay the paper into position. Turn the kite over, glue the outer flaps, and tuck them over the perimeter strings. Flaps (Diagram 3) should be cut out of the tissue, folded in half, and glued to the head-stick string. These flaps will cause a buzzing sound when the kite is flying.

The flying bridle is shown in Diagram 4. This kite must be flown with a long tail which can be made of strips of old cloth attached to a loose string run between the bottoms of the C sticks—the stronger the breeze, the longer the tail.

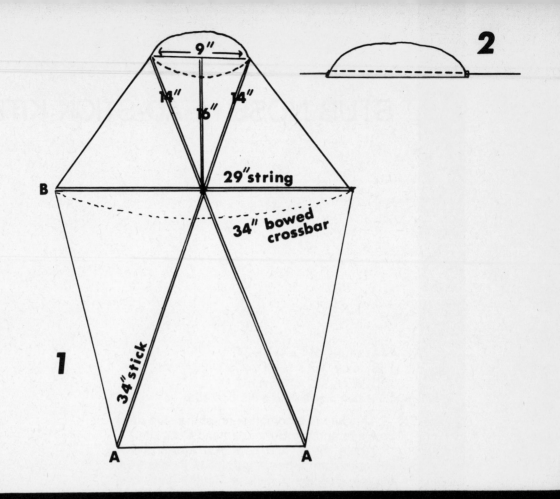

**1**

9″

14″   16″   14″

B

29″string

34″ bowed crossbar

34″stick

A          A

**2**

**3**

**4**

# STUB NOSE HEAD-STICK KITE

2 (A) sticks, ½″ x ¼″ x 34″
1 (B) stick, ⅜″ x ¼″ x 34″
1 (C) stick, ⅜″ x ¼″ x 16″
1 14-inch piece of flexible bamboo

This kite is a combination of the stub nose bow kite and the Bermuda head-stick kite.

Notch the A and B sticks. Attach the A sticks to each other at a point 14 inches from the top. Bow the B stick so that the taut string tied from tip to tip of the bow measures 29 inches and attach the cross string to the point where the A sticks cross. Pivot the A sticks from the crossed point so that the top points of the A sticks spread 9 inches.

Then fix the base of the C stick (the modified head-stick) to the same cross-point with a small nail and insert the bamboo into the tops of the A sticks, bowing it toward the front of the kite. Tie the C stick firmly to the midpoint of the bowed bamboo.

Before covering the kite, move the bowed cross stick (B) into flying position facing directly out from the frame. Then tie a string completely around the outside perimeter of the kite frame from stick-end to stick-end. Fit thin tissue or paper as tightly as possible over the kite frame, leaving ½ inch flaps extending beyond the framing string. Fold the flaps over the string and glue firmly into position.

A paper flap (Diagram 3) similar to the hummer on the Bermuda kite can be folded over the string at the top extending between the tops of the A sticks. The bridle for this kite is shown in Diagram 4. Strings must run from each of the six stick ends and meet at a point approximately 6 inches in front of the kite's center cross point.

# BASIC BOX KITE

4 (A) sticks, ¼″ x ⅜″ x 40″
4 (B) sticks, ¼″ x ½″ x 17″
2 wide strips of light cloth or paper, 12″ x 51″

Lay the strips of covering material parallel to each other and mark the sheets 3 inches from the left side. Make three additional marks at 12-inch intervals across the sheets leaving 12 inches between the farthest right (fourth mark) and the end of the strips.

Cut ¼-inch wide notches in the ends of the B sticks. Also cut ⅛-inch deep and ½-inch-wide notches at the midpoints (Diagram 2) of the B sticks. This makes it possible to lock them together when they are put into position bracing the kite frame.

With the marks lined up on the paper strips, spread the sheets 24 inches between the inside edges , taking care to keep the strips parallel to each other. Glue the narrow edge of the individual A sticks to the covering at the 12-inch marked intervals. When the sticks are firmly glued to the covering, spread glue on the outside of the 3-inch-wide left-hand flap. Fold the 12-inch right flap over until it completely covers the left flap and glue the flaps together. When the glue is dry, fit the B sticks into position (Diagram 1) and tie the crossed units together.

**1**

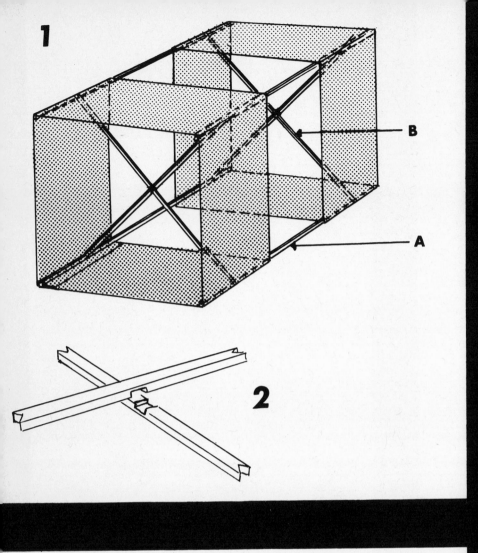

B

A

**2**

**3**

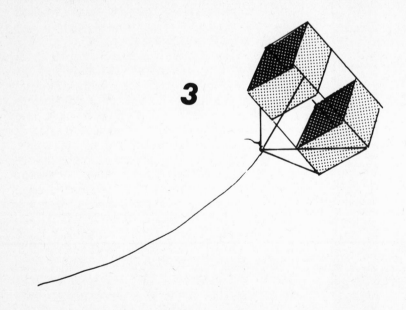

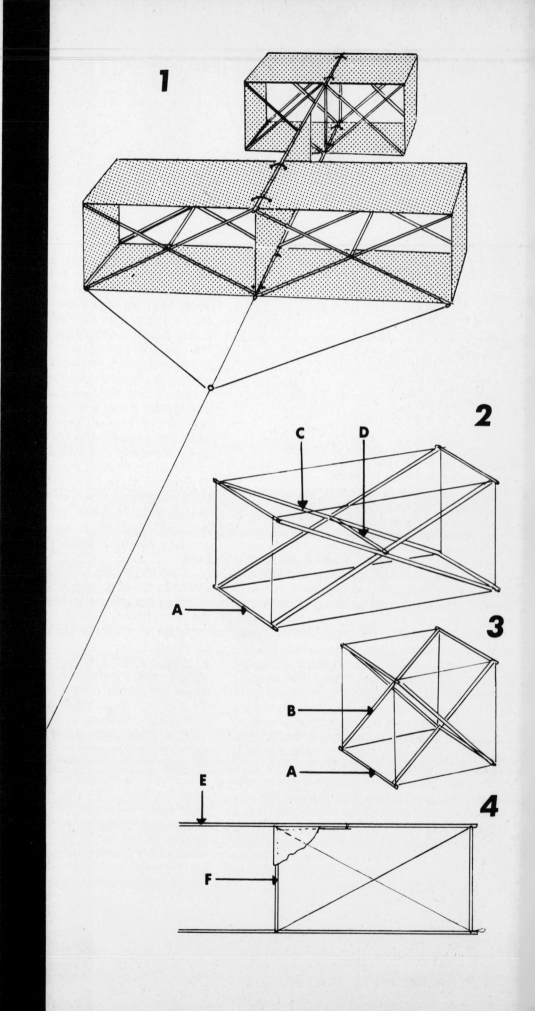

# MINIATURE NAVY BARRAGE KITE

16 (A) sticks, 3/16″ round x 9¾″
8 (B) sticks, ¼″ round x 16¾″
8 (C) sticks, ¼″ round x 26½″
2 (D) sticks, ¼″ round x 9¾″
2 (E) sticks, ⅜″ x ⅜″ x 36″
2 (F) sticks, ⅜″ x ⅜″ x 9″

Each wing is made up of four C sticks (the struts), four A sticks (longerons), and a single D stick (tie-red). Mark the midpoint of the C sticks and fasten the sticks into four pairs with small nails. Spread the pairs slightly to form X's and fasten them to the longerons (A sticks) with glue or small nails. Then attach the tie-rod (D) between the pairs of struts (C sticks) with strong thread or light fishing line. In order to hold the struts rigidly in position, strong cord or 10-pound test monofilament should be looped around the construction as shown in Diagram 2. It is best to make shallow notches near the tips of the longerons in order to hold the cords. Then seal them with glue.

The two tail sections (Diagram 3) are constructed exactly like the wings. Make the barrage kite's flat body (Diagram 4) with two E sticks and two F sticks. Crossed diagonal cords give added strength to the body frame. Drive a small nail or tack into the front of the top E stick to keep the wings in place when they are added to the frame.

Cover the top, bottom, and one end of each wing section and each tail section with light paper or cloth. Cut the covering sheets ½ inch wider than the space they are to cover. This allows edges that can be folded around the cords. Seal the edges (flaps) with glue to both the struts and longerons. Cover the body by gluing the paper or cloth to the struts and strings as shown in Diagram 4.

Two holes must be punched into the top and bottom of each wing section and the top and bottom of each tail section, 1½ inches from the edge that will butt up against the body. Reinforce the edges of the holes with glue in order to avoid tearing. Cords (Diagram 1) must be slipped through the holes to hold the kite together. Four are used to fasten the tail sections together (both top and bottom surfaces). Four more lines pass through the same holes and attach the tail section to the body.

Coat the edges of the wing sections that attach to the body with strong glue. Place the wings against the body, thread strings through the precut holes (two on each individual wing surface), and tie the strings tightly together (Diagram 1).

Attach a flying bridle as shown in the illustration, reaching from the outside bottom point of each wing and from the bottom body stick. Tie the lines to a ring or loop and attach the flying line to the ring or loop.

It is almost impossible to launch this kite alone. Have someone hold the kite at the end of about 50 feet of cord, pointing it up at approximately a 45-degree angle. Pull the line fairly taut and, after signaling the kite-holder to release the kite, begin a short run. The kite should rise immediately and continue to climb as line is fed out. If the kite moves on too horizontal a plane, it may fall into a dive. This can be taken care of by adding small 1-ounce weights to the tail as necessary.

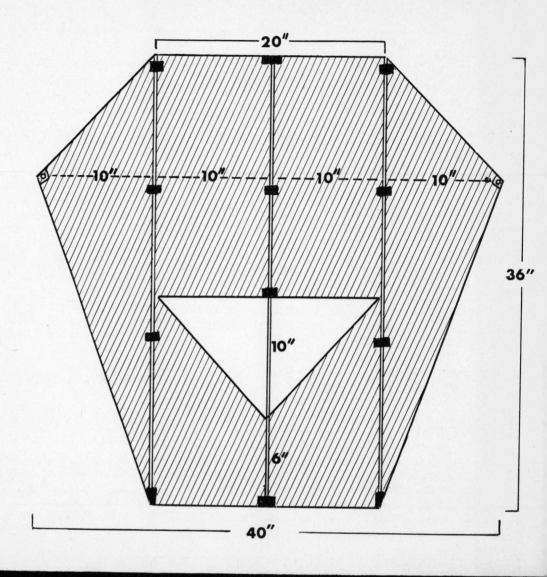

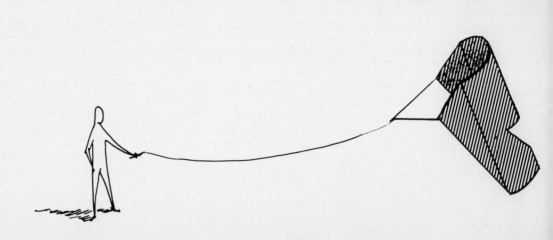

# SCOTT SLED

3 (A) sticks, ⅜" round x 36"
1 sheet of plastic or polyethylene, 36" x 40"

Cut the sheet exactly as shown in Diagram 1. Take particular care to get the triangular vent centered on the sheet. Place glue on the sticks and press them into place. Then run a strip of reinforced tape around the perimeter of the kite to prevent the fabric from fraying or tearing, and lay small strips of tape over the sticks as shown in the illustration. Punch holes in the tips of the "wings" and reinforce the edges of the holes with glue or light tape. The bridle line attaches to the two holes and should extend 72 inches. The flying line is tied to the midpoint of the bridle line.

The Scott Sled is extremely easy to launch and requires no running. Simply feed it out at first by hand and then let it pull the string out at its own pace.

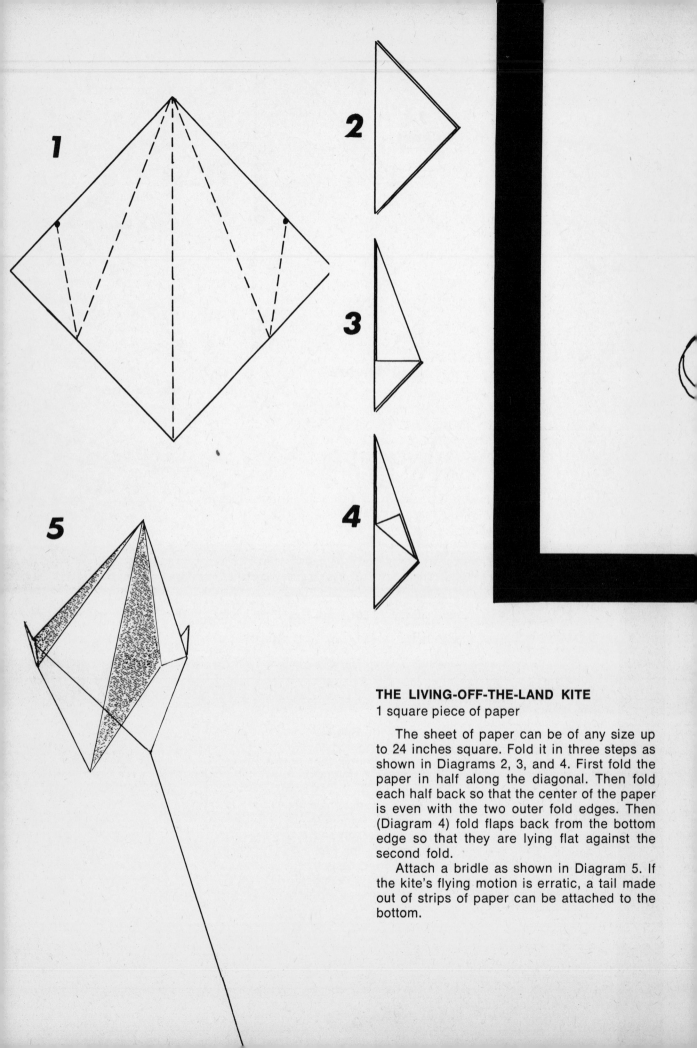

**1**

**2**

**3**

**4**

**5**

## THE LIVING-OFF-THE-LAND KITE
1 square piece of paper

The sheet of paper can be of any size up to 24 inches square. Fold it in three steps as shown in Diagrams 2, 3, and 4. First fold the paper in half along the diagonal. Then fold each half back so that the center of the paper is even with the two outer fold edges. Then (Diagram 4) fold flaps back from the bottom edge so that they are lying flat against the second fold.

Attach a bridle as shown in Diagram 5. If the kite's flying motion is erratic, a tail made out of strips of paper can be attached to the bottom.

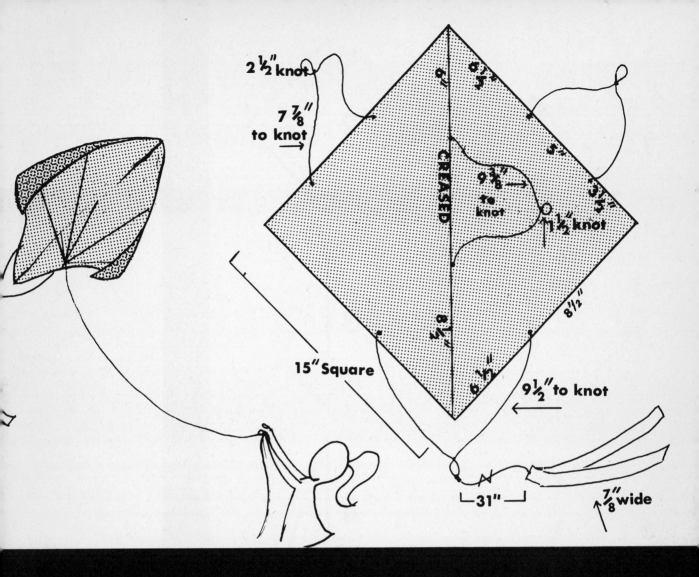

# BASIC PARA-WING

16″ square of light cloth

This is a simplified variation of the Rogallo Para-Wing, and although difficult to rig, it flies beautifully. The flying angle, or tilt into the wind, must be maintained at approximately 15 degrees. Hem the cloth ½ inch, leaving a 15 inch square. Then attach strings exactly as shown in Diagram 1, and press a fold into the fabric along the diagonal. The length and weight of the tail will be dictated by the prevailing winds. Bring the three looped-rigging strings together and tie them with the flying line. The kite is then ready to be hand-launched.

**Credits for Illustrations:** Mac Brewer—pp. 14, 15, 20. *The News*—p. 25 bottom. Acme—pp. 38, 39. United Press International Photos—pp. 48 left and top three at right, 50 left and center, 51 right and bottom, 53 bottom. Wide World Photos—pp. 48 bottom two at right, 49, 66 top. Mabel Hubbard Bell, Courtesy and Copyright, National Geographic Society, 73 inset. The Bell Family and National Geographic Society, 72–73.